What Is the Evidence for Social Inflation?

Trends in Trial Awards and Insurance Claim Payments

LLOYD DIXON, NICHOLAS M. PACE, JAMES DAVIDSON, JAMIE MORIKAWA

RAND SOCIAL AND ECONOMIC WELL-BEING

For more information on this publication, visit **www.rand.org/t/RRA2645-1**.

Published by the RAND Corporation, Santa Monica, Calif.

Library of Congress Cataloging-in-Publication Data is available for this publication.

ISBN: 978-1-9774-1349-9

Cover image: Adobe Stock/suphakphen

About This Report

Social inflation is a term that has been used to describe social and behavioral trends that are said to expand the liability of parties allegedly responsible for harms and their insurers. Although there is a great deal of discussion and debate regarding social inflation and its purported causes, there is not a great deal of empirical research on whether social inflation is actually occurring. In this report, we look for trends in litigation rates, trial awards, and insurance claim payments that are consistent with the expected effects of social inflation. Our aim is not to identify causes for social inflation but rather to determine whether there is evidence that social inflation is occurring.

The RAND Kenneth R. Feinberg Center for Catastrophic Risk Management and Compensation

The Feinberg Center, part of the Justice Policy Program within RAND Social and Economic Well-Being, seeks to identify and promote laws, programs, and institutions that reduce the adverse social and economic effects of natural and manmade catastrophes by improving incentives to reduce future losses; providing just compensation to those suffering losses while appropriately allocating liability to responsible parties; helping affected individuals, businesses, and communities to recover quickly; and avoiding unnecessary legal, administrative, and other transaction costs.

Questions or comments about this report should be sent to the project leader, Lloyd Dixon (dixon@rand.org). For more information about the Feinberg Center, see https://www.rand.org/well-being/justice-policy/centers/catastrophic-risk-management.html or contact the director at ccrmc@rand.org.

Institute for Civil Justice

The RAND Institute for Civil Justice (ICJ) is dedicated to improving the civil justice system by supplying policymakers and the public with rigorous and nonpartisan research. Its studies identify trends in litigation and inform policy choices concerning liability, compensation, regulation, risk management, and insurance. The Institute builds on a long tradition of RAND research characterized by an interdisciplinary, empirical approach to public policy issues and rigorous standards of quality, objectivity, and independence. ICJ research is supported by pooled grants from a range of sources, including corporations, trade and professional associations, individuals, government agencies, and private foundations. All its reports are subject to peer review and disseminated widely to policymakers, practitioners in law and business, other researchers, and the public. The ICJ is part of the Justice Policy Program within RAND Social and Economic Well-Being. The program focuses on such topics as access to justice, policing, corrections, drug policy, and court system reform, as well as other policy concerns pertaining to public safety and criminal and civil justice. For more information, email justicepolicy@rand.org.

Funding

Funding for this research was provided by the generous contributions of the RAND Institute for Civil Justice Advisory Board and the RAND Kenneth R. Feinberg Center for Catastrophic Risk Management and Compensation Advisory Board.

Acknowledgments

We would like to thank ALM for providing access to the extensive civil trial verdict report holdings available through Law.com's VerdictSearch. We would also like to thank Verisk for providing data on trends in the frequency and severity of insurance claims by accident year for several first-party and third-party market segments, and recognize James Davidson, senior actuarial director—commercial lines at Verisk, for taking a great deal of time to explain Verisk's claims database and statistical methods. Eric Helland, senior economist at RAND and professor of economics at Claremont McKenna College, and James Lynch, owner of James Lynch Casualty Actuary and former chief actuary of the Insurance Information Institute, provided thorough and very insightful peer reviews of multiple drafts of this report. Members of the ICJ and Feinberg Center advisory boards also provided helpful comments on the final draft. James Anderson, director of the Justice Policy Program and ICJ, provided much-appreciated advice over the course of the project. Finally, the report was very skillfully edited by Stephanie Lonsinger.

Summary

Social inflation is a term that has been used to describe social and behavioral trends that expand the tort liability of parties allegedly responsible for harms and their insurers. Use of the phrase in this manner goes back to the 1970s when Warren Buffett described social inflation as "a broadening definition by society and juries of what is covered by insurance policies."[1] In recent years, insurers have also used the term to describe the specific factors that they claim are driving rapid and unexpected increases in the costs of claims on liability policies.

Insurers and others have argued that social inflation creates a feedback loop in which rising levels of tort compensation fuel expectations of financial windfalls among potential claimants and the attorneys who represent them, which, in turn, stimulates the filing of new claims and associated lawsuits. Social inflation's claimed expansion of liability would presumably result in higher compensation for lawsuits that are settled, an increased likelihood that plaintiffs will prevail at trial, and higher trial awards. The specter of higher tort verdicts and settlements would then put upward pressure on insurance claim payments, regardless of whether the claim was disputed in court.

For many stakeholders, social inflation is an unwelcome development that threatens the insurance industry and can cause economic disruption. According to one observer, social inflation is "one of the biggest disruptors facing the insurance industry."[2] For others, social inflation is a positive development, better enabling injured parties to receive the compensation they deserve. Still others question whether social inflation is occurring at all.

Although there is a great deal of discussion and debate regarding social inflation and its purported causes, there is not a great deal of publicly available empirical research on whether social inflation is actually occurring. In this report, we look for trends in litigation rates, trial awards, and insurance claim payments that are consistent with the expected impacts of social inflation. Specifically, we address the following research questions:

- Have tort filings in state courts increased?
- Has the percentage of verdicts that result in monetary awards to the plaintiffs (*plaintiff win rate*) increased?
- Have trial awards increased faster than the rate of economic inflation, and how have any such increases varied by case characteristics?
- Has insurance claim severity (measured as dollars per claim) increased faster than economic inflation, and how have the changes compared with trends in trial awards?

---

[1] Warren Buffett, "Chairman's Letter—1977," Berkshire Hathaway, March 14, 1978.

[2] Claire Wilkinson, "Social Inflation Keeps Rising for Insurers: Panelists," *Business Insurance*, January 17, 2020, as quoted in Jim Lynch and Dave Moore, *Social Inflation and Loss Development*, Casualty Actuarial Society and Insurance Information Institute, 2022, p. 3.

Increases in trial awards and insurance claim severity net of economic inflation would be suggestive of social inflation but would not necessarily provide conclusive evidence. The difference between the growth rates in trial awards or claim severity and economic inflation could be due to social inflation, as well as factors external to the civil justice system. Examples of such other factors include changes in medical practice patterns, changes in injury severity, and changes in the mix of injuries for which insurance claims are filed or litigation initiated.

Research Approach

We turned to ALM's Law.com VerdictSearch unit for data on jury verdicts. VerdictSearch provided us with data on 37,668 verdicts between 2010 and 2019, and we determined that 26,114 of those were personal injury and wrongful death (PI/WD) verdicts, which were relevant to this analysis. We chose this ten-year window because we believed that VerdictSearch's ability to gather verdict information was relatively stable during this period and because it was a time when the topic of social inflation was repeatedly discussed in insurance industry publications. Ending the analysis in 2019 avoided potential issues related to any impacts of the COVID-19 pandemic.

Our analysis of trends in the frequency of tort lawsuits relied on data from the National Center for State Courts (NCSC). We used data from the 19 states that have tracked net tort filings in their general jurisdiction courts for at least one decade in a manner consistent with NCSC standards for reporting caseloads. We augmented these data with data from California, which was not one of the 19 states included in the NCSC database.

Verisk (formerly known as Insurance Services Office, or ISO) provided data for our analysis of trends in insurance claims. Verisk maintains one of the largest databases in the world on insurance policies and claims. It currently collects some 4 billion detailed records each year on insurance policies and claims from insurers. According to Verisk's website, these data represent 70 to 75 percent of the premium volume for commercial insurance lines in the United States and about one-third of the premium for personal lines.

We adjusted trial awards for inflation using the Bureau of Economic Analysis's personal consumption expenditure price index (PCEPI). To examine the sensitivity to the results to changes in the quantity of health care consumed and not just the price, we used an index of annual medical expenditures per capita in the United States. For the analysis of insurance claim severity, we used the following PCEPI components: weighted average, medical care, motor vehicle repair and maintenance, and motor vehicle parts and accessories, with the weights dependent on the insurance market segment under consideration.

Findings

Court Filings per Capita Increased in State Courts

The annual number of new tort case filings per capita rose about 10 percent between 2012 and 2019 in 19 states for which data were available. What is unknown is whether this increase is due to factors associated with social inflation or other factors, such as an increase in underlying tortious incidents. However, the decline in the nationwide frequency of insurance claims reported below is inconsistent with such an explanation. Further research is needed to understand the factors that pushed up filings per capita during this period, but the increase in case filings potentially supports the contention that social inflation is occurring.

Plaintiff Win Rates in Cases That Reached a Verdict Increased

We found that the plaintiff win rate increased from 53 to 64 percent between 2010 and 2019, which is consistent with the narrative about the potential effects of social inflation. One possible mechanism that could lead to such an increase is delayed defense response to changes in case values. If defendants are not making settlement offers that are keeping up with rising settlement values, cases that plaintiffs will win might go to trial that would have settled otherwise. Over time, defense strategy may adapt, and the plaintiff win rate might return to previous levels. Other factors, such as a decrease in the likelihood that defense verdicts are reported to VerdictSearch, could potentially explain part or all of the increase. Although such a hypothesis is plausible, further research is needed to establish the extent to which such factors have actually had an impact.

Inflation-Adjusted Trial Awards Increased

We found that trial awards in PI/WD cases grew faster than the rate of inflation over the study period. The first row of Table S.1 shows that, after adjusting for inflation, trial awards per plaintiff grew at a 7.6-percent compound annual growth rate (CAGR) between 2010 and 2019 while controlling for case characteristics. We examined the sensitivity of these results to differing assumptions meant to capture changes in the quantity of health care provided in addition to price. Under plausible assumptions, we did not find that the results changed a great deal.

In addition, we found that the percentage of awards that are large (i.e., at least $5 million) increased during the study period. As shown in Figure S.1, the percentage of large awards (in 2019 dollars per plaintiff) ranged from 5.5 to 7.5 percent between 2010 and 2016, but that percentage began to increase in 2017, reaching just under 12 percent by 2019.

These results suggest that social inflation is not constant but ebbs and flows. For trial awards as a whole, we found that inflation-adjusted awards per person started to increase in 2014. This finding is consistent with information from other sources. Specifically, during the course of this project, several insurers and other informed parties with whom we spoke believed that social inflation accelerated in the mid-2010s. Internet search counts also indi-

TABLE S.1

CAGRs for PI/WD Inflation-Adjusted Trial Awards per Plaintiff

			CAGR (%)	
Case Type	CAGR 2010–2019	Year Growth Rate Increased	Pre-Dividing Point	Post-Dividing Point
All plaintiff wins	7.6***	2014	−3.8*	8.0***
Organizational defendants	7.3***	2016	1.2	8.7***
Commercial trucking	8.5***	2018	−0.1	19.1***
Other commercial vehicles	5.1***	2017	2.8	6.2***
Medical malpractice	5.7**	2018	1.0	12.4***
Other cases against organizational defendants	8.8***	2014	−4.3	9.6***
Non-organizational defendants	8.3***	2014	−2.5	8.6***
Private auto	8.3***	2014	−0.7	8.4***
Other cases against non-organizational defendants	8.1**	2016	−4.2	9.3**

NOTE: *N* = 15,017 trial awards. * = statistically different from 0 with 90-percent probability; ** = statistically different from 0 with 95-percent probability; *** = statistically different from 0 with 99-percent probability.

FIGURE S.1

Trends in the Percentage of Inflation-Adjusted PI/WD Trial Awards That Are Large

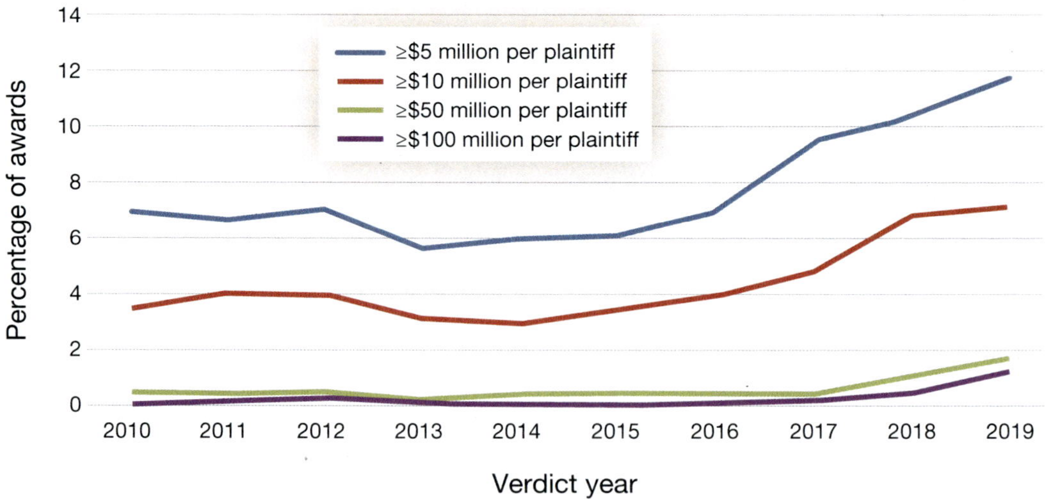

NOTE: *N* = 15,017 trial awards. We defined a *large* award as at least $5 million. Awards and cutoffs are shown in 2019 dollars.

cated that concern about social inflation picked up at this time. Using the Google Books Ngram Viewer, we found that the term "social inflation" dropped in usage during the Great Recession of 2008 and began increasing in 2014.[3] Google internet searches for "social inflation" using a custom date range yielded a modest number of results from 2000 to 2012 before jumping in number in 2014. Two very large verdicts in 2014 were perhaps the catalyst for increased attention that year.

These findings provide evidence that social inflation is occurring, but they are not necessarily conclusive. For example, declines in the percentage of cases that go to verdict or in the percentage of plaintiff verdicts that are reported to VerdictSearch could cause the awards for the verdicts in our dataset to increase, even absent social inflation.

The increase in trial awards beginning in 2014 corresponds to an uptick in the percentage of trial awards in which brain injuries were alleged in the underlying cases. The increase could be due to several factors, such as a change in the injury severity in cases that ultimately make it to trial; an improved ability to detect and treat brain injuries; or an increased willingness of juries to acknowledge less serious forms of brain injury. We found that the increased frequency of brain injuries contributed to the growth in trial awards between 2010 and 2019, but that contribution was modest.

Contrary to expectations, we did not find evidence that social inflation affected organizational defendants to a greater degree than non-organizational defendants.[4] Annual growth rates in trial awards were of similar magnitudes for verdicts against both types of defendants. However, we did not consider the organization's size in our analysis. It could be that trial awards grew more rapidly for larger organizations than smaller ones. Juror beliefs that non-organizational (i.e., individual) defendants are backed by large insurance companies could also explain the lack of difference.

We found some support for the notion that the impacts of social inflation vary by case type. Although the differences in CAGRs across case types are not particularly pronounced (as shown in Table S.1, they vary from 5.1 to 8.8 percent), differences in the timing of the CAGR increases are more noteworthy. Faster growth appears to have begun sooner for private auto cases and cases in the *other cases against organizational defendants* category. The later increase in awards for commercial trucking is surprising given all the attention paid to this sector, but the growth rate for this case type in the last two years of the study period is the highest observed.

The results also suggest that social inflation is not occurring equally in all states. The largest increases in trial awards and the earliest onset of faster growth occurred in New York, California, New Jersey, and Texas. Smaller increases and later onset dates were observed in

---

[3] The Google Books Ngram Viewer is a tool that yields the yearly count of user-defined text strings found in Google's scientific literature–focused collection of books and magazines (Google Ngram Viewer Team, "About Ngram Viewer," webpage, undated).

[4] *Organizational defendants* refers to businesses, government agencies, nonprofits, and other types of organizations.

Pennsylvania, Illinois, and Florida. There was a much lower increase in trial awards in the remaining states when taken together, although larger effects in some states could be offset by smaller effects in others.

The Inflation-Adjusted Severity of Insurance Claims Involving Bodily Injury Increased

The inflation-adjusted severity of bodily injury (BI) insurance claims rose at a CAGR of approximately 2.7 percent between 2010 and 2019 for claims brought under commercial liability policies that predominantly have limits equal to $1 million per occurrence and $2 million in aggregate (shown as $1 million/$2 million) and for claims brought under personal auto policies with limits that usually do not exceed $100,000/$300,000 (see Table S.2). We refer to these limits as *baseline policy limits*. We found that the pattern of annual growth also lines up with that for trial awards in PI/WD cases. In both situations, there was little growth between 2010 and 2013 and faster growth from 2014 through 2019. This finding provides some initial evidence that the increase in claim severity is driven at least in part by social inflation.

The CAGR for BI claims between 2010 and 2019 for these lower-limit policies was less than one-half that for trial awards (2.7 percent versus 7.6 percent). The procedures that Verisk uses to calculate claim severity may be, in part, due to this difference. Namely, data from the previous five to seven years are used to develop reported losses, which means that if social inflation is accelerating, it may only gradually be reflected in the calculated claim severities for the 2010–2019 period. The claim severities reported are based typically on policies held

TABLE S.2
CAGRs for the Inflation-Adjusted Severity of Commercial Liability and Personal Auto Claims for Baseline Policy Limits

	CAGR (%)	
Market Segment	**2001–2010**	**2010–2019**
BI claims	2.0[a]	2.7
CGL, premises and operations	0.9	4.3
CGL, products and completed operations	4.7	1.7
Third-party personal auto	—	2.0
Third-party commercial auto	0.5	3.0
Property damage (PD) claims		
Including personal auto	—	3.5
Excluding personal auto	0.9	3.8

NOTE: This table shows rates for claims brought under commercial liability policies with limits that are typically $1 million/$2 million and claims brought under personal auto policies with limits that usually do not exceed $100,000/$300,000. CGL = commercial general liability.

[a] Excludes personal auto.

by small- and medium-sized firms. We also found that severity was increasing more rapidly for policies with higher limits and that, in some market segments, these growth rates were similar to those for trial awards. This result can be interpreted in different ways. On the one hand, it could indicate that social inflation affects higher-limit policies and the larger firms that typically hold them to a greater degree than lower-limit policies. On the other hand, it could suggest that social inflation affects policies with all limits equally but that increasingly binding limits reduce the growth rate that is observed for lower-limit policies. In this latter case, it could be that policyholders with lower limits experience the same social inflation as policyholders with higher limits, but they see constrained growth in insured losses that is offset by higher growth in uninsured losses.

Contrary to expectations, we found only limited evidence that the growth rates for PD claims were lower than those for BI claims. The growth rates were similar for the baseline policy limits; however, it could be that increasingly binding limits for both types of claims hampered the difference in growth rates. Two findings provide some support for the notion that PD claims were not affected by social inflation to the same extent as BI claims. First, we observed no upswing in severity growth rates for PD claims that correspond to the increase in trial awards beginning in 2014. Second, in contrast to the other market segments considered, we found less growth in claim severity for higher-limit policies when property damage accounted for a larger share of the overall claim payments.

Insurance Claim Frequency Decreased, Offsetting to Some Extent Any Impact of Social inflation on Loss Ratios

Insurance claim frequency fell for all market segments considered between 2001 and 2010 and for all market segments except third-party commercial auto BI claims between 2010 and 2019. The overall decline in frequency between 2001 and 2019 was large enough to nearly or fully offset the increase in severity over that period for all the market segments considered.

Social inflation could lead individuals to seek compensation for injuries more frequently when an injury occurs, thus increasing the frequency of insurance claims. However, increased safety regulation can reduce the underlying injury rate. By increasing liability costs, social inflation itself can also induce potentially responsible parties to improve safety practices and reduce the underlying injury rate. Thus, even if the likelihood that an injured party would seek compensation or file an insurance claim is increasing, the overall number of claims could be declining if the underlying injury rate is falling. Consequently, a decline in insurance claim frequency does not mean that social inflation is not occurring. Instead, such a decline suggests that social inflation will not necessarily manifest as an increase in observed loss ratios or insurance premiums. It could be the case, however, that loss ratios and premiums would have declined more rapidly absent social inflation.

The decline in claim frequency contrasts with the increase in tort filings per capita. One potential explanation for the increase in filings per capita is that the underlying tortious incidents are increasing. The decline in claim frequency provides some support for the hypothesis that the increase in tort filing per capita is driven, at least in part, by social inflation and not primarily by an increase in underlying tortious incidents.

Implications

Our findings provide evidence consistent with an upsurge in social inflation during the 2010s. We did not attempt to formally isolate social inflation from other factors that could be causing inflation-adjusted trial awards and insurance claim severity to increase. As discussed above, there are several plausible, competing explanations for each of the observed trends.

Further work in various areas is needed to help improve our understanding of whether social inflation exists and its magnitude:

- The statistical power of our insurance claim analysis is limited by having access to only average claim severity across all claims in a given year by market segment. Additional insights and precision in the estimate of the consequences of social inflation would likely be gained by using claim-level data.
- An understanding of the trends in claim frequency and severity for higher-limit policies, including those in the excess and surplus lines markets, would improve insight into whether social inflation is affecting larger firms more than smaller firms.
- An examination of the relationship between changes in claim severity and the tort regime or tactics of the plaintiffs' attorneys in each state could also prove a fruitful area for analysis. Variation in tort standards, damage caps, and litigation practices by the plaintiffs' bars across states and their changes over time could help better isolate and quantify the effects of social inflation.
- Further investigation of how best to control for changes in medical practice patterns and the price and quality of vehicle replacement parts would provide more confidence on the extent to which increases in trial awards and claim severity are caused by social inflation or to factors external to the tort system.

The findings in this report add to evidence that social inflation has occurred in some insurance lines. Concluding that social inflation exists is not an assessment of whether social inflation is good or bad—that will depend on the factors driving it. For example, one could argue that an increase of trial awards because jurors are ignoring the law or insurance contract language is a negative driver of social inflation. Conversely, elimination of a cap on noneconomic damages by legislative action could be viewed as a positive driver consistent with broader public will. A next step in the assessment of social inflation would be to gain a better understanding of the factors that are driving it and whether these factors serve broader social goals.

Contents

Figures and Tables

Figures

Tables

CHAPTER 1

Introduction

Social inflation is a term that has been used to describe social and behavioral trends that expand the tort liability of parties allegedly responsible for harms and their insurers. Use of the phrase in this manner goes back to the 1970s when Warren Buffett described social inflation as "a broadening definition by society and juries of what is covered by insurance policies."[1] In recent years, insurers have also used the term to describe the specific factors that they believe are driving rapid and unexpected increases in the costs of claims on liability policies.[2]

Although similar, the definitions of social inflation offered by insurance industry–related organizations have varied in focus. The Swiss Re Institute, for example, argues that social inflation "describes the impact of changes in the tort system through which most insurance liability cases are settled."[3] The Geneva Association defines social inflation as "legislative and litigation developments that impact insurers' legal liabilities and claims costs."[4] And the Insurance Research Council (IRC) describes social inflation as a "recent growth in liability risk and costs" because of several litigation factors, including

- rollbacks of previously enacted tort reforms
- changes in underlying beliefs about the appropriateness of filing lawsuits and expectations of higher compensation
- increasing numbers of very large jury verdicts, reflecting an increase in juries' sympathy toward plaintiffs and in their willingness to punish those who cause injury to others.[5]

---

1 Warren Buffett, "Chairman's Letter—1977," Berkshire Hathaway, March 14, 1978.

2 See Sangmin Oh, "Social Inflation," Social Science Research Network, 2021, p. 2, for data showing a steep rise in references to social inflation in 2018 and 2019 by the 15 largest commercial automobile liability groups during conference calls. According to Oh, references to social inflation were very low between 2008 and 2017.

3 Swiss Re Institute, "Social Inflation: A Building Pain Point in US Liability Insurance," *Economic Insights*, No. 21/2019, November 14, 2019, p. 9.

4 Darren Pain, *Social Inflation: Navigating the Evolving Claims Environment*, Geneva Association, December 2020, p. 6.

5 IRC, *Social Inflation: Evidence and Impact on Property-Casualty Insurance*, June 2020, pp. 1–2.

As is apparent from this sample of definitions, social inflation is used to refer both to changes in the tort system and to the consequences of those changes. Taken together, such definitions essentially describe a situation in which the liability of parties potentially responsible for tort-related losses (e.g., automobile drivers for highway collisions, manufacturers for product-related injuries, store owners for falls on slippery floors) has expanded from what was traditionally the case.

In this report, we use *social inflation* to refer to expanded liability risk for potentially responsible parties and their insurers. As shown in Figure 1.1, changes in tort doctrine, the propensity of injured parties to sue, juror attitudes, and attorney trial strategy, as well as growth in third-party litigation funding and attorney advertising, might all be considered *potential drivers* of expanded liability. The *potential consequences* of such expanded liability could include an increased number of tort claims brought against individuals and organizations, a decreased likelihood that such claims will be denied in their entirety, increased levels of compensation when claims are paid, an increased frequency in tort litigation when claims are not resolved, increases in the rates at which plaintiffs in tort cases win at trial, and increases in the average awards.[6]

The potential consequences of expanded liability can themselves act as drivers of social inflation. For example, increasingly large jury awards in tort trials could have the secondary effect of increasing settlement values for similar tort claims that may never reach the litigation stage.[7] Another example might be an increased win rate for plaintiffs at trial that in turn influences how often claims adjusted by liability insurers are paid.

---

[6] In this report, we use the term *claim* to refer to any demand presented to an individual or entity for monetary compensation for alleged losses (such as those arising from physical injuries, property damage, or fraudulent actions) based on a theory of tort liability. Such individuals or entities (often described generically as *potentially responsible parties* or *alleged tortfeasors*) can choose to ignore the claim, overtly refuse to pay at all, agree to pay the requested compensation, or offer to compromise on a reduced amount. When alleged tortfeasors have tort liability coverage as part of an insurance policy, the insurer will likely decide how to respond to the claim, and it will be the insurer, not the alleged tortfeasor, who will pay any compensation up to the level of the policy limits. Some claims may involve the filing of a civil lawsuit with the intent of receiving a judicial determination of the right to such compensation, and some of those lawsuits may reach the point where a trial is held and the questions of liability and the size of any monetary award are addressed. If an award is granted by the trier of fact (often a jury but sometimes the judge overseeing the litigation) against a defendant with liability insurance coverage, it will also be paid to the level of the policy limits (with the defendant responsible for any excess judgment). Defendants without liability insurance coverage will be fully responsible for any adverse trial awards. Therefore, it is important to remember that not all claims involve lawsuits, not all lawsuits involve trials, not all claims involve insurers, and insurer payments for tort liability claims (whether or not a trial award is involved) do not fully capture all payments arising from all tort claims.

[7] Insurance claims are often settled using software that considers similar claims. If the data trend upward, the settlement offers will trend upward. This practice can impact claims, even without attorney representation.

FIGURE 1.1
Social Inflation Terminology

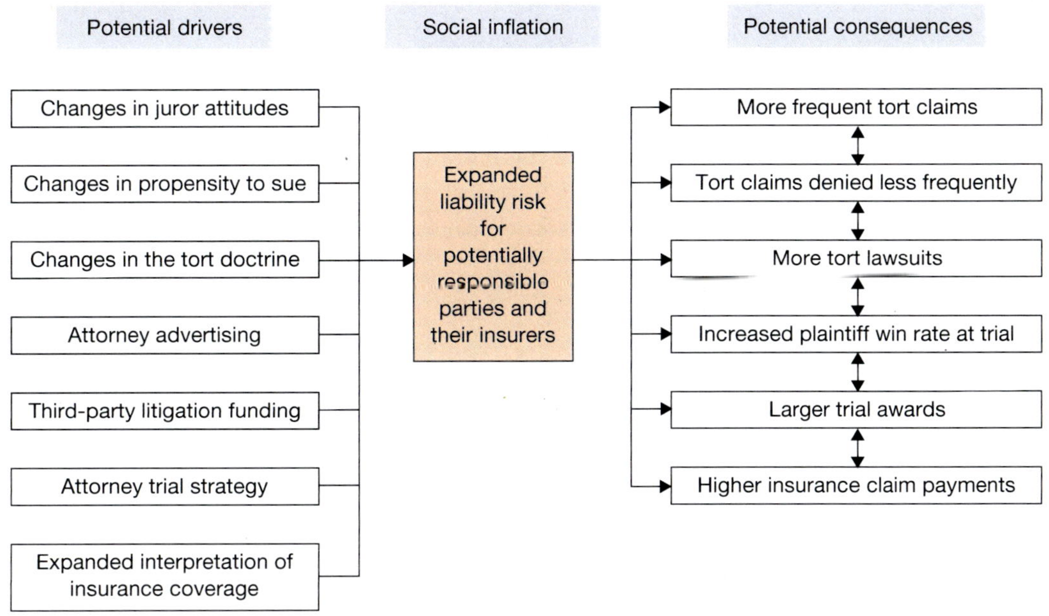

For many stakeholders, social inflation is "one of the biggest disruptors facing the insurance industry."[8] For others, social inflation is a positive development, better enabling injured parties to receive the compensation they deserve. Still others question whether social inflation is occurring at all.[9]

Although there is a great deal of discussion and debate regarding social inflation and its purported causes, there is not a great deal of publicly available empirical research on whether social inflation is actually occurring. In this report, we look for trends in litigation rates, trial awards, and insurance claim payments that are consistent with the purported impacts of social inflation during a period in which many observers asserted that the U.S. civil justice system was experiencing social inflation.[10] To this end, we investigate the extent to which trial

[8] Claire Wilkinson, "Social Inflation Keeps Rising for Insurers: Panelists," *Business Insurance*, January 17, 2020, as quoted in Jim Lynch and Dave Moore, *Social Inflation and Loss Development*, Casualty Actuarial Society and Insurance Information Institute, 2022, p. 3.

[9] J. Robert Hunter, Joanne Doroshow, and Douglas Heller, *How the Cash-Rich Insurance Industry Fakes Crises and Invents Social Inflation*, Consumer Federation of America and the Center for Justice and Democracy at New York Law School, March 2020.

[10] It should be noted that some who use the term social inflation appear to be referring to a general expansion of liability for *all* civil claims and not just those associated with tort-related losses. In this view, compensation paid for breaches of contract, for example, would also be increasing as a result of certain societal, behavioral, and legal trends. In this report, however, we focus on tort claims because the historical usage of

awards and the severity of insurance claims (measured as dollars per claim) have increased faster than the rate of economic inflation.

Increases in trial awards and claim severity net of economic inflation would suggest social inflation, but they would not necessarily provide conclusive evidence. As illustrated in Figure 1.2, the difference between the growth rates in trial awards or claim severity and economic inflation could be due to social inflation, as well as factors external to the civil justice system. Examples of such factors include changes in medical practice patterns (such as the number or types of procedures ordered), changes in injury severity, or changes in the mix of injuries for which insurance claims are made or litigation initiated. In this report, we provide data on the sum of components 2 and 3 in Figure 1.2, which we refer to as *inflation-adjusted growth* in either trial awards or insurance claim severity.[11]

To explore the empirical evidence for social inflation during our study period, we address the following research questions:

- Have tort filings in state courts increased?
- Has the percentage of tort verdicts that result in monetary awards to the plaintiffs (*plaintiff win rate*) increased?
- Have tort trial awards increased faster than the rate of economic inflation, and how have any such increases varied by case characteristics?
- Has insurance claim severity (measured as dollars per claim) increased faster than economic inflation, and how have the changes compared with trends in trial awards?

Our analysis of verdicts is based on more than 26,000 reported verdicts across the United States between 2010 and 2019. As we discuss in Chapter 2, a previous study has reported data on verdicts, but that analysis was restricted to verdicts with trial awards greater than $1 million, and the number of verdicts used in the analysis was not disclosed. Our analysis of insurance claims is based on millions of claims between 2001 and 2019, offering a more direct analysis of insurance frequency and severity than in previous studies.

We are not able to isolate social inflation from other factors that affect the growth of trial awards and claim severity. However, growth in the inflation-adjusted trial awards and claim payments is suggestive of social inflation, and the patterns that we observe over time and the types of trial awards and insurance claims most affected can provide some additional insight into the extent to which changes are driven by social inflation as opposed to factors external to the tort system. We also do not speculate on whether social inflation, if it exists, is good

the term (i.e., in the context of the U.S. civil justice system) appears to have been primarily concerned with liability for harms to persons or property.

[11] Stakeholders sometimes refer to the sum of categories 2 and 3 as social inflation. This broader measure of social inflation includes all factors that cause the growth in jury verdicts or insurance claim severity to exceed economic inflation, including changes in medical practice patterns and vehicle technology. See, for example, the Geneva Association's "broad interpretation" of social inflation (Pain, 2020, p. 8). Our use of *social inflation* corresponds more closely with the Geneva Association's narrow definition.

FIGURE 1.2
Decomposition of Changes in Trial Awards and Insurance Claim Severity

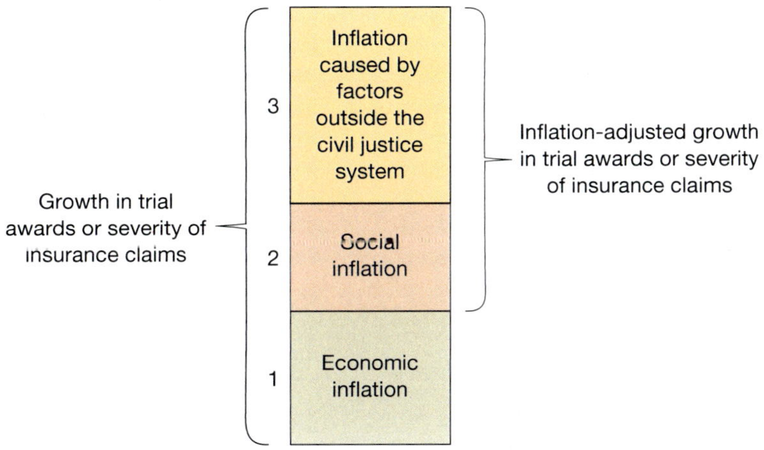

or bad. That determination will rest, in part, on what factors are driving social inflation. For example, growth in liability because jurors are ignoring the law or the coverage language in insurance policies might be viewed negatively, while growth in liability because of the removal of noneconomic damage caps by a state legislature might be viewed positively as consistent with public will.

Organization of This Report

The remainder of this report is organized into seven chapters and two appendixes:

- **Chapter 2, Potential Drivers and Consequences of Social Inflation,** provides background on the potential drivers and consequences of social inflation and reviews prior research on the effect of social inflation on insurance claims.
- **Chapter 3, Analytic Approach,** describes the litigation, verdict, and insurance claim data used in the analysis; metrics used to characterize trends in trial awards and insurance claims; and price indices used to adjust for economic inflation.
- **Chapter 4, Litigation Trends,** examines trends in the number of tort cases filed per capita, the share of cases that reach verdict, and the plaintiff win rate.
- **Chapter 5, Ten Years of Trial Awards,** presents findings on the trends in personal injury or wrongful death (PI/WD) trial awards between 2010 and 2019, then examines trends by case type, claimed harm, and state in which the verdict was reached.
- **Chapter 6, Trends in Insurance Claim Severity,** investigates whether changes in the inflation-adjusted severity of insurance claims are consistent with the expected effects of social inflation.

- **Chapter 7, Trends in Insurance Claim Frequency and Loss Ratio,** examines changes in the number of claims brought during the period over which the policy is in effect (claim frequency) and the implications for change in the loss ratio (the product of claim frequency and claim severity) and insurance premiums.
- **Chapter 8, Implications,** provides final observations on whether the empirical evidence we have collected is consistent with the expected effects of social inflation, as well as priorities for future research.
- **Appendix A, Statistical Methods and Sensitivity Analysis,** describes the statistical methods used in the analysis and the sensitivity of the results, excluding the relatively small number of trial awards that are far larger than other awards in the sample. It also examines the sensitivity of key results to the price indices used in the analysis.
- **Appendix B, Additional Statistics on Verdicts and Trial Awards,** shows how the mix of case types for the verdicts analyzed in this report has changed over the study period and the mean and median trial awards by case type.

CHAPTER 2

Potential Drivers and Consequences of Social Inflation

The concerns voiced by the insurance industry in the mid-1970s and in the decades that followed were not focused on the relationships between insurers and their insureds. Rather, they related to claims brought against those insureds by individuals or entities seeking monetary compensation for alleged tort-related harms that the insureds would be legally responsible for as a result of applicable legislation and judicially developed case law. Such demands to be compensated in accordance with prevailing law are often characterized as *third-party liability claims* because they involve insurance policies that protect insureds from the financial responsibilities arising from allegations of tort harms asserted by those who were not parties to the insurance contract.[1]

To be more concrete, a third-party insurance policy for *commercial liability coverage* (sometimes referred to as commercial general liability [CGL] insurance) could protect a grocery store from tort claims arising from customer injuries resulting from a failure to clean up spilled milk in the dairy aisle, while a policy for *motor vehicle liability coverage* (commonly referred to as personal auto insurance) could protect the driver of an automobile from tort claims arising from the driver's failure to yield to oncoming traffic when making a left turn. Such liability policies do not prevent such claims from being made, but instead, they ensure that all or part of the monetary compensation provided to a third party making a successful claim would be paid out of the insurance policy rather than the pockets of the insured.

Not all personal injuries, deaths, or property damage resulting from supermarket falls, auto accidents, defective products, medical treatment errors, or other causes result in liability claims against a person or an entity, such as a business or government agency (such persons or entities are known as *alleged tortfeasors*). Those who incur these losses may decide that no one else was responsible for the incident or that the effort to present a claim would not be worth the possible compensation. They may consult with legal counsel and be advised that the applicable legal standards for making a successful tort claim under the circumstances

[1] The term *third party* refers to the tort claimant as opposed to the liability policy's first party (the policyholder) and second party (the insurer). In contrast, *first-party coverage* provides coverage for property damage or other losses suffered by the insured. Examples include coverage for wind or flood damage on a homeowner's policy or coverage for theft on a personal auto policy.

surrounding the incident were not favorable, or that the transactional costs associated with advancing the claim were of a magnitude that would present a significant risk of financial loss if success were not certain. When claims are made against an alleged tortfeasor, they alert their liability insurer. The insurance company (which then essentially takes over the defense of any tort claim) may assess that the applicable facts or law would support a decision to decline any payment, or it may offer an amount that it considers will fully compensate the injured party (i.e., make "whole"), based on the facts presented and an understanding of insurer obligation under the policy. Moving up the claiming pyramid, a claimant who rejects the insurer's offer could file a formal lawsuit to seek a trial verdict in their favor. In the context of tort claims involving personal injuries or wrongful death, however, such lawsuits are typically initiated only after an attorney has agreed to represent the claimant on a *contingency* basis (i.e., the fee for legal services is calculated as a percentage of compensation obtained for the client). Because of the risk borne by the attorney in such arrangements, counsel must perceive the claim as financially viable after factoring in the potential fee in light of the likelihood of any recovery. These recoveries can be in the form of an award based on a verdict at trial (*trial award*), but they much more frequently result from a settlement of the claim before or after a trial.

Such considerations were at the heart of assertions that social inflation had resulted in an expansion of tort liability. In some sense, however, the development of the law related to tort liability has always been in an expansion phase, as the following examples show:

- The middle years of the 20th century, for example, were marked by an increasing liberalization of the legal standards for seeking compensation as a result of injuries caused by defective products. Legal doctrine in this area slowly evolved from viewing such incidents simply as contractual problems in which the sole remedy was the replacement or refund of the item involved in the injury to holding manufacturers liable for unreasonably dangerous products, even if such products worked exactly as designed.
- The same period also saw a movement away from doctrines that prevented any tort recovery at all if the person incurring the alleged injuries was judged to have played a role in the incident, even if only a trivial one, to a more balanced view in which recovery would be reduced proportional to the claimant's relative fault.
- In a similar move toward expansion, actions seeking compensation for the wrongful death of a family member historically could only recover damages related to the survivor's expectations of future monetary benefits, such as financial support. But over time, damages for more-intangible losses (e.g., premature interruption of family closeness or the warmth of feeling between family members) could be obtained as well.
- An even earlier example of expansion involved the liability of an employer for the acts of its employees. The 19th century rule limited a company's tort liability to acts of employees that were expressly assented to by the employer (which would not include intentional bad acts), but in the ensuing decades, employer liability could be imputed if the employee's actions were reasonably foreseeable in light of the duties assigned by the employer.

The above examples describe once-denied types of harms that are now eligible for compensation, once-protected types of parties that could now be liable to pay a successful claim for compensation, and increases in the amount of compensation available for certain types of loss. In other words, tort liability has already been expanded.

But the purported expansion of liability that the insurance industry has been worried about since the 1970s is based not only on developments in tort law. It also concerns supposed shifts in behavior of the key actors involved in every step of the tort resolution process. Reading through news articles and research reports about tort-related social inflation from the 1970s to recent times, we found the following assertions about the disruptive effects of social inflation:

- Individuals who are hurt in an accident are said to be ever quicker to point the finger at others as the cause of their injuries, the alleged value of the claims they make are growing compared with similar incidents in the past, and they are more likely to seek the assistance of legal counsel at every stage of the resolution process.
- Attorneys in the business of representing tort claimants are said to be asking for more compensation on behalf of their clients, are less likely to accept reasonable offers from insurers to settle claims, and are more inclined to file a lawsuit to seek a judicial determination of the claim rather than continuing to seek an informal compromise.
- Attorneys are also said to be increasingly aggressive in advertising for clients, accepting funding from third parties, and accepting new cases that they might have declined in the past because of questionable facts or law.
- Judges who oversee such litigation are said to be increasingly receptive to the arguments of the attorneys representing the plaintiffs in these cases, and they are less likely to follow prior precedent and long-standing judicial practices intended to treat both plaintiffs and defendants equally and fairly.
- If the case reaches the trial stage, jurors are believed to be increasingly likely to rule in favor of the plaintiffs and award damages at levels higher than seen in the past for the same types of claims, particularly when the alleged tortfeasor is perceived to be a large organizational entity.
- Jurors are said to be more likely than ever before to award plaintiffs sums of money that are wildly disproportional to the facts of the case and the controlling law. Some attribute this to plaintiff trial tactics grounded in what is referred to as "reptile theory," a trial strategy that focuses more on juror fears and emotions than on the reason and logic behind the argument.
- If the matter goes to appeal, appellate court justices are said to be less likely to overturn lower court decisions that were favorable to the plaintiff and more likely to make new laws that place those who must defend tort claims brought against them (or their insureds) at a disadvantage.
- And in light of these behavioral shifts, insurance adjusters evaluating new claims and the legal counsel who are charged with the responsibility of defending those claims

that have morphed into lawsuits are said to be settling more often and for more money because of fears of substantial financial and reputational liabilities that could result from an adverse verdict at trial.

Not every commentator claims that all these hypotheses are true, but it has been asserted that the sum of these multiple changes creates a feedback loop in which rising levels of tort compensation fuel expectations of financial windfalls among potential claimants and the attorneys who would represent them, which in turn stimulates the presentation of new claims and the filing of associated lawsuits that further adds to the cycle.

There is a lot to unpack in these assertions, but at their core, the expansion of liability warned of by the insurance industry would presumably result in unpredictable increases in claim payments, which in the aggregate would result in continued growth in the overall amount of distributed compensation (at least that distributed by liability insurers) at a rate greater than what might be expected as a result of *price inflation* (i.e., increases in the general level of prices for goods and services). To the extent that any such increases in expected payouts have not been factored into the premiums that insurers charge for liability coverage for incidents that might occur during current or future policy years, social inflation would indeed have a disruptive effect on insurer profits and financial stability. And, to the extent that the expansion in liability is captured in insurance premiums, consumers are adversely affected by higher prices of insurance, as well as more-expensive goods and services generally.

Examining objective indicators of possible social inflation influences is the obvious place to start any inquiry into whether social inflation exists at all. Initially focusing on the social and behavioral shifts that are claimed to be the underlying causes of expanded liability, such as whether those who might be called to serve as jurors are increasingly hostile toward large corporate entities, would, by itself, provide little in the way of evidence that social inflation is occurring and is an issue worthy of policymakers' attention. Unless it can first be systematically documented, for example, that litigation arising out of such claims is becoming more likely, that average trial awards are rising faster than would be expected given price inflation, or that payments per insurance claim are trending upward at speeds that cannot be explained by factors external to the civil justice system, discussions about beliefs and actions of actors within the civil justice system and their possible effects on a changing legal environment are, at best, premature and, at worse, avoid examining more important foundational issues.

Prior Empirical Research

In a 2022 study, Lynch and Moore found evidence of social inflation in claim severity in certain insurance lines.[2] They based their conclusions on loss-development triangles that can be constructed using data that insurers provide to the National Association of Insurance

[2] See Lynch and Moore, 2022, p. 13.

Commissioners (NAIC). Loss-development triangles show how the claim costs for a given accident year grow over time. For example, loss-development triangles can be used to calculate the ratio of claims paid through 24 months to the amount paid through 12 months, the ratio of claims paid through 36 months to the amount paid through 24 months, and so forth. An increase in these link ratios for subsequent accident years is taken as evidence of social inflation. Lynch and Moore analyzed loss-development triangles for both paid and incurred losses.

This approach has limitations. Accelerating general economic inflation would cause the link ratios to increase, even in the absence of social inflation. Thus, estimates based on this approach could overstate the effects of social inflation. However, Lynch and Moore pointed out that the relatively slow and steady inflation over the period examined in their analysis reduces concern about this factor. The approach could also understate the effects of social inflation if claims paid in the initial year grew substantially for more-recent accident years, while the ratio of claims paid in subsequent periods to the initial 12 months remained stable.

Lynch and Moore focused on commercial auto liability insurance from 2000 through 2018, and they found evidence of social inflation for this insurance line. They estimated that social inflation potentially caused commercial auto liability claim payments to be roughly 14 percent (or $20 billion) higher between 2010 and 2019 than they would have been otherwise. Lynch and Moore also found evidence of social inflation for medical malpractice and occurrence-based policies in NAIC's "other liability" line.[3]

Lynch and Moore examined the personal automobile liability line, the claims-made policies in the other liability line, and the occurrence-based product liability line. They concluded that, although their approach did not provide evidence of social inflation in these lines, it also did not rule out the existence of social inflation. For example, they suspected that social inflation was having a significant impact on other liability claims-made policies and hypothesized that large random variation was overwhelming any social inflation signal.

IRC based its analysis of social inflation on trends in industry-aggregate incurred claim losses from 2007 through 2019.[4] Trends in these incurred losses reflect changes in both the frequency and severity of claims. IRC found that incurred losses grew faster than the general rate of inflation between 2013 or 2014 (depending on the available data) and 2018 in the following insurance lines:

- commercial auto liability
- medical malpractice
- products liability
- other liability.

[3] Most insurance policies that are included in the *other liability* line are sold to businesses or to individuals providing professional services. CGL coverage is an example of the type of insurance included in this line.

[4] IRC, 2020.

The amount by which the growth in losses exceeded the economic inflation rate varied by line. The difference was greater for commercial auto liability than for the other examined insurance lines: Claims grew at a 10.9-percent annualized rate between 2013 and 2018, while the consumer price index grew at a 1.5-percent annualized rate. Although growth in industry-aggregate incurred losses that exceeds general inflation may well be consistent with social inflation, other factors could also cause such growth. The IRC analysis does not account for change in the overall size of the economy, which would affect the number of policies issued, the number of miles driven, and industry-aggregate incurred losses. The results could also be due, in part, to changes in factors other than social inflation, such as standards of medical care.

Sangmin Oh investigated the effects of social inflation on insurance prices. Using a database of insurance rate filings, Oh compared commercial and personal auto liability insurance prices before and after the 2015 settlement of a high-profile lawsuit pertaining to a Walmart truck that crashed into a vehicle, in which comedian Tracy Morgan and five others were killed or seriously injured.[5] Oh, in effect, used personal automobile insurance prices as a control in his analysis of the social inflation on the commercial auto market because previous research has suggested that corporate defendants are more exposed to social inflation risk than individual defendants. He compared price growth before and after the settlement of the Tracy Morgan suit, which Oh posited is "widely known as a watershed moment for social inflation."[6] Oh found that commercial auto insurance rates grew about 2 percent faster than personal auto insurance rates after 2015, providing evidence that social inflation had increased commercial auto insurance rates. Oh's method for identifying the effect of social inflation is rigorous but still has potential weaknesses. For example, it may not be able to fully control for differences across lines in insurer pricing strategies and does not isolate changes in frequency from changes in claim severity.

In a December 2021 report, the Swiss Re Institute presented data on median U.S. trial awards for vehicle negligence and general liability cases by year between 2010 and 2019. The analysis was restricted to awards of greater than $1 million. The share of these verdicts that exceeded $5 million was also reported annually over the same period. The Institute found that the median award grew by approximately 25 percent between 2010 and 2019. The percentage of large verdicts (i.e., $5 million or more) also grew between 2010 and 2019. However, it does not appear that these results were adjusted for economic inflation, and the number of verdicts underlying the analysis was not disclosed. The Institute linked the increase in trial awards to a rapid increase in insurance claim losses, stating that the effect was most pronounced on "large corporate risk in the umbrella and excess liability space, commercial auto,

---

[5] Oh, 2021. Oh also used variation in insurance rate growth across states that were more and less exposed to large verdict awards to identity a social inflation effect. The Tracy Morgan settlement was reported in 2015 ("Walmart Settles Tracy Morgan Lawsuit After Deadly Crash with Company Truck," *The Guardian*, May 27, 2015).

[6] Oh, 2021, p. 5.

medical malpractice and directors & officers."[7] The report does not present information on insurance claim cost but rather illustrates the consequences of the alleged increase in claim costs on the *combined ratio* (i.e., the ratio of incurred claim losses and insurer expenses to the insurance premium, multiplied by 100) for the general liability, medical malpractice, and commercial auto liability lines. The authors noted that the combined ratio had been more than 100 (corresponding to negative underwriting profits) between 2014 and 2020 for medical malpractice and general liability and that the combined ratio had been more than 100 between 2011 and 2020 for commercial auto liability. The authors found that "[p]ricing in all liability lines has climbed in response to rising concerns about adverse reserve development and social inflation."[8] The outcome measures used by the Swiss Re Institute present some complexity when interpreting the findings. The combined ratio is a function of both losses and premiums, and high combined ratios could indicate that the policies were inadequately priced rather than the consequence of growing claim costs. Similarly, a focus just on prices, without attempting to control for confounding factors, could lead to incorrectly attributing price increases to social inflation when other factors are responsible.

Other analysts have come to different conclusions regarding evidence of social inflation. Hunter, Doroshow, and Heller examined trends in losses paid and losses incurred in several property casualty market segments. Their analysis is based on industry-aggregate data and covers 1999 through 2018. They concluded that after adjusting for inflation, population growth, and miles driven, insurance claims "have stayed generally flat or increased relatively little" over this period. Drawing on these findings, they concluded that "the existence of 'social inflation' is contradicted by all evidence."[9] In their view, social inflation is a marketing term created by the insurance industry to justify rate increases. A limitation of their analysis is that it is unable to distinguish changes in the frequency of insurance claims from the severity of claims. Social inflation could potentially be driving increases in claim severity, which is largely offset by declines in claim frequency.

This study brings new data to bear on the issue of social inflation in two ways. First, we analyze more than 26,000 verdicts between 2010 and 2019 from across the United States. Our analysis is not limited to trial awards that exceed $1 million, although we analyze the percentage of overall awards that are large (i.e., at least $5 million). Second, we take advantage of more-direct data on insurance claims, using statistics based on millions of claims. Furthermore, the statistical data do not conflate claim cost and policy premium information and allow us to analyze claim frequency separately from claim severity. The data used in our analysis and the methods that we used to analyze them are described in the next chapter.

---

7 Swiss Re Institute, *U.S. Litigation Funding and Social Inflation: The Rising Costs of Legal Liability*, December 2021, pp. 13–14.

8 Swiss Re Institute, 2021, p. 15.

9 Hunter, Doroshow, and Heller, 2020, pp. 2–3.

CHAPTER 3

Analytic Approach

We begin this chapter by describing the data that underlie our analysis of insurance claims. As discussed in Chapter 2, these claims sit near the bottom of the claiming pyramid. We then discuss the rationale for using tort filings and trial verdicts to understand the possible impacts of social inflation on the overall compensation process before turning to the case filing and trial verdict data used in the analysis. Finally, we introduce the price indices used to account for changes in general price levels.

Insurance Claim Data

Verisk (formerly known as Insurance Services Office, or ISO) maintains one of the largest databases in the world of insurance policies and claims. It currently collects some 4 billion detailed records each year on insurance policies and claims from insurers. According to Verisk's website, these data represent 70 to 75 percent of the U.S. insurance industry premium volume for commercial insurance lines and about one-third of industry premiums for personal lines in 2022.[1] Verisk uses this information to calculate the claim frequency, severity, and loss ratios for various types of insurance policies, among other analytical purposes. Insurers use this information in setting insurance rates and seeking approval for their rates from state insurance regulators.

Verisk provided us with data on trends in the frequency and severity of insurance claims by accident year for several first-party and third-party market segments.[2] In most cases, Verisk was able to provide annual data from 2001 to 2020. Table 3.1 lists these market segments, such as commercial general liability (CGL) or personal auto liability, and whether the claims in the market segment were brought predominantly under occurrence policies or

[1] Verisk, "Information from the Verisk Database," webpage, undated. These market share statistics pertain primarily to coverage written in the admitted insurance market.

[2] Verisk did not provide data on individual claims but rather statistics on the average severity and frequency by accident year. *First-party insurance* provides coverage for losses directly suffered by the insured (the first party), which are predominantly caused by property damage. *Third-party (or liability) policies* provide coverage for losses suffered by parties other than the insured because of the insured's actions. The third party will often file a legal action to recover costs from the insured. Third-party claims can involve both property damage and bodily injury.

TABLE 3.1
Insurance Lines Examined in This Analysis

Verisk Market Segment	Predominant Policy Type	NAIC Line Number	NAIC Line Description
Third-party claims			
CGL—products and completed operations	Occurrence	18.1 17	Product liability—occurrence Other liability—completed operations
CGL—premises and operations	Occurrence	Part of 17.1	Other liability—occurrence
Commercial auto	Occurrence	19.4	Commercial auto liability—other
Personal auto	Occurrence	19.2	Private passenger auto liability—other
First-party claims			
Commercial property (excluding catastrophic events)	Occurrence	5.1	Commercial multiple peril—non-liability portion
Commercial auto	Occurrence	21.2	Commercial auto physical damage
Personal auto	Occurrence	21.1	Private passenger auto—physical damage

SOURCE: Features information from NAIC, "Uniform Property & Casualty Product Coding Matrix," January 1, 2024.

claims-made policies.[3] By way of explanation, CGL coverage protects businesses from tort claims for personal injuries, deaths, property damage, and certain other losses, such as those from misleading advertising, libel, or invasion of privacy. The claimed liability could arise from a company's services, products, or operations or from the acts of its employees, but CGL does not cover professional negligence, such as physician malpractice. CGL is usually divided into two types: (1) *premises and operations*, which provides coverage for incidents that have occurred on the company's premises or as a function of its operations, and (2) *products and completed operations*, which provides coverage related to the company's products or completed work.

Also listed in Table 3.1 are the NAIC lines to which the Verisk policy categorizations most closely correspond, although, as can be seen, mapping between Verisk market segments and NAIC lines is not always straightforward. Verisk did not include data on claims brought under the no-fault provisions for automobile insurance that exist in many states when calculating the statistics used in this analysis. Similarly, uninsured and underinsured motorist claims are not included. Verisk data also do not include bad-faith claims brought by policyholders against insurers.

[3] *Claims-made policies* cover claims that are made during the policy period, regardless of when the loss actually occurred. *Occurrence policies* cover losses that occur during the policy period, regardless of when the claim is filed.

To provide a feel for the considerable number of claims that underlie the data in this report, Table 3.2 lists the number of claims between 2001 and 2020 on which our analysis of claim severity is based.[4]

A wide variety of businesses are represented in the Verisk data, as reflected by the roughly 1,200 business types (or classes) that Verisk uses to categorize them. The majority of claims for commercial lines in the Verisk database are brought under policies held by small-sized and medium-sized businesses. There are a few very large businesses, such as oil refineries, in the Verisk database, but not many. Table 3.3 provides examples of the distribution of policyholders by size for a few of the exposure bases used by Verisk for general liability policies. As shown, the median firm payroll for an exposure base measured using payroll is $57,200, with

TABLE 3.2
Number of Claims in Verisk Data on Which Severities Are Based

Market Segment	Claims from 2001 to 2020 (millions)
Third-party claims	
CGL, premises and operations	3.6
CGL, products and completed operations	0.7
Commercial auto	8.9
Personal auto	41.1
First-party claims	
Commercial property[a]	1.8
Commercial auto	6.7
Personal auto	77.7

SOURCE: Features information from Verisk data.
NOTE: Includes claims closed with or without payment.
[a] Excludes catastrophic events.

TABLE 3.3
Policyholder Size for Selected Exposure Bases in the Verisk Database

Exposure Base	10th Percentile	50th Percentile	90th Percentile	99th Percentile
Gross sales ($ thousands)	29.2	379	3,110	22,900
Payroll ($ thousands)	13.6	57.2	479	2,300
Number of students[a]	14	66	320	932

SOURCE: Features information from Verisk data.
NOTE: These data include general liability and premises and operations claims.
[a] Used for policyholders whose size is best characterized by number of students.

[4] These data could not be restricted to the 2010–2019 period of our analysis.

the payroll of firms in the 99th percentile at $2.3 million. For comparison, the average payroll of the approximately 6 million firms in the United States with employees was $1.12 million in 2017, and after excluding the 20,000 firms with 500 or more employees, the average payroll of the remaining 5.98 million firms was approximately $450,000.[5]

Verisk staff estimate that 80 to 90 percent of the commercial policies in its database have a $1 million limit per occurrence and a $2 million aggregate limit.[6] There are much higher limits in the data—for example, $50 million and even higher—but they are few. The policy limits for the personal auto bodily injury (BI) claims in the Verisk database vary widely by state because of minimum financial requirements. For states with a $25,000 per person and $50,000 per incident minimum limit, the most common policy limits are $25,000/$50,000 (38 percent of policies) and $100,000/$300,000 (28 percent of policies). For states with a $30,000/$60,000 minimum BI limit, the most common limits are $50,000/$100,000 (30 percent) and $100,000/$300,000 (45 percent).[7]

Metrics Used to Characterize Trends in Claim Severity, Frequency, and Loss Ratio

Claim Severity

Claim severity measures the average loss payment, including allocated loss adjustment expenses, per claim.[8] It refers to the size of claim payments, not the severity or seriousness of the underlying injury. Average severities reported by Verisk include both claims closed with payment and those closed without payment. Insurers report to Verisk every quarter on every claim that was closed during the reporting period or those that were still open at the end of that period. Insurers report both paid and outstanding losses (*outstanding* in this context describes an insurer's best estimate of what will subsequently be paid on the claim). *Incurred losses* on a claim are defined as the sum of paid loss, outstanding loss, and actual and estimated remaining allocated loss adjustment expenses. Therefore, incurred losses reflect the insurer estimate of how much claim costs will increase as a result of social inflation or other factors during the life of the claim. Over time, an increasing percentage of claims for a given accident year are closed, and as a consequence, the incurred claim severity data for that year will increasingly reflect the actual and final amount paid on the claim as opposed to the insurer estimate of an outstanding loss.

---

5 These comparison values are taken from Lloyd Dixon and Jamie Morikawa, *Improving the Availability and Affordability of Pandemic Risk Insurance: Projected Performance of Proposed Programs*, RAND Corporation, RR-A1223-1, 2021, p. 28, based on U.S. Census Bureau data.

6 These limits are not adjusted over time to account for economic inflation.

7 Data were provided by Verisk on February 23, 2022.

8 *Allocated loss* adjustment expenses are associated with adjusting insurance claims that can be attributed to a particular claim. They contrast with *unallocated loss* adjustment expenses, which are insurers' expenses related to adjusting claims that cannot easily be allocated to individual claims.

Verisk *develops* the losses of the insurer-provided claims data. This process uses past data on the difference between the reported incurred losses and the ultimate paid losses. Such development addresses any systematic errors in insurer estimates of incurred losses for reported claims, as well as growth in the number of claims for a given accident year that are observed over time. Verisk typically uses data from the prior five to seven years to develop losses, which assumes that prior-year social inflation continues during the remaining life of the claim. It also means that if social inflation is accelerating it may only fully manifest in the claim severity data for a given year once enough time has passed for the actual payments on the claims to be largely complete. In a period of accelerating social inflation, estimates based on the most recent severity data might then be low. The reverse is true if social inflation were decelerating.

Verisk's severity statistics do not consider deductibles paid by the policyholder or losses that might be incurred by the policyholder above the policy cap. Thus, an increase in the deductible over time could in principle cause Verisk's severity figures to decline. However, Verisk staff do not consider any such effects as significant. For example, Verisk staff estimate that only roughly 10 percent of CGL policies have deductibles. Similarly, an increase in the policy limit over time could cause reported severities to increase even if there had been no underlying change in actual losses. Verisk staff also do not consider any such effect as significant over the period examined.

Table 3.4 shows the average claim severities between 2010 and 2019 for the market segments examined in this analysis.

Claim Frequency

When analyzing changes in claim frequency over time, Verisk starts with a measure of the exposure base for each type of policyholder. For example, when the exposure base is measured by annual sales, Verisk might calculate the number of claims during the policy period per $1,000 of sales. For an educational institution, it might calculate the number of claims per student. To combine data across different exposure bases, Verisk calculates the number of claims per million dollars of premium earned. This is referred to as *nominal frequency*. Nominal frequency, however, may not be well suited to examine changes in frequency over time. For example, if frequency remained constant at one claim per $1,000 of sales but general prices (including premiums) doubled, then nominal frequency would halve. To control for such changes, Verisk calculates the *on-level frequency*. To calculate on-level frequency, premiums in past years are brought up to what they would have been had the policy been written in the current year.[9] To account for the gradual appearance of claims for a given accident year over time, Verisk also *develops* the frequency using the same process described for claim severity. There are sometimes challenges in determining what the premium of a policy would

[9] Using current insurance rate schedules to calculate on-level frequency means that the current assessment of underlying risk, including any increases over time caused by social inflation, would be embedded in the premium, which is the denominator of the on-level frequency.

TABLE 3.4
Average Claim Severity Between 2010 and 2019 for Market Segments Analyzed

Market Segment	Dollars per Claim (thousands of 2019 dollars)
Third-party BI claims	
CGL, premises and operations	56.2
CGL, products and completed operations	65.7
Commercial auto	66.6
Personal auto	20.5
Third-party property damage (PD) claims	
CGL, premises and operations	17.8
CGL, products and completed operations	39.9
Commercial auto	5.3
Personal auto	3.6
Third-party commercial auto (includes BI and PD)	
Trucks, tractors, and trailers	20.5
Personal passenger vehicle types	16.8
First-party PD claims	
Commercial property[a]	48.8
Commercial auto	6.0
Personal auto	3.0

SOURCE: Features information from Verisk data.
NOTE: Includes claims closed with or without payment.
[a] Excludes catastrophic events.

be had it been written in the current accident year, which can reduce confidence that changes in on-level frequency reflect actual frequency changes.

Loss Ratio

Recall that the loss ratio is the product of claim frequency and claim severity and is expressed as loss divided by premium. To analyze changes in the loss ratio over time, we used the *on-level loss ratio*, which is the product of on-level frequency and severity. Paralleling the construction of severity, loss is measured as insured loss, which ignores the deductible and any losses above the policy limit. Increases in the loss ratio put pressure on insurers to raise the premiums at which they offer coverage. Conversely, decreases in loss put downward pressure on insurance prices.

Litigation Data

Rationale for Examining Lawsuits

In this report, we examine two important subsets of liability claims: those that have evolved into lawsuits seeking tort damages and those that eventually result in a verdict at trial (typically, but not always, the result of a jury decision).[10] At first blush, the idea of focusing on trial verdicts or even litigation generally to help understand possible systemwide changes as a result of social and behavioral shifts makes little sense. Although comprehensive insurance industry information on the likelihood of litigation is not readily available, it is clear that not all liability claims involve the initiation of a civil tort lawsuit. One insurer's estimate of the proportion of general liability claims brought against its insureds that ultimately resulted in litigation was 35 percent, though other sources indicate a much lower percentage.[11] We do know, however, that state court tort lawsuits rarely reach the trial stage. Studies of multiple jurisdictions suggest that 5 percent would be a comfortable upper bound on the percentage of tort cases that are resolved by trial.[12] And about one-half of those resolutions are in favor of the plaintiffs.[13] Thus, a rough back-of-the-envelope estimate is that roughly 0.88 percent of liability claims ultimately result in a plaintiff verdict.

So what can less than 1 percent of all tort liability claims provide in the way of evidence about the possible social inflationary impacts on the overall system? Cases reaching the trial stage would certainly not be typical of tort claims generally. Except in instances in which relatively minor tort claims (typically for property damage only) evolve into lawsuits in small claims courts, where applicable rules and common practices encourage (or even require) plaintiffs to proceed without counsel, tort-related litigation is likely to be filed with attorney

---

[10] Verdicts can also result from *bench trials* (i.e., trials in which the judge presiding over a case also serves as the trier of fact to decide liability and, if necessary, damages, in the same way a jury would). The most comprehensive nationwide data available on the types of trials held in tort cases are now almost 20 years old, but those numbers suggest that nine out of ten trials involve juries as the triers of fact (see Table 1, "Civil Trials in State Courts, by Case Type, 2005," in Lynn Langton and Thomas H. Cohen, *Civil Bench and Jury Trials in State Courts, 2005*, Bureau of Justice Statistics Special Report, U.S. Department of Justice, October 2008, revised April 9, 2009, p. 2).

[11] "The Hartford Reports: More Than 40 Percent of Small Businesses Will Experience a Claim in the Next 10 Years," The Hartford, March 30, 2015. Also see Sedgwick, "Liability, Litigation Trends, Drivers and Strategies," 2022, which asserts that in the areas of general liability and automobile liability, less than 1 percent of claims involve litigation.

[12] Cases ending with an adjudicated disposition (which include jury trials, bench trials, directed verdicts, and arbitrations) comprised about 3 percent of all tort resolutions (see Table 5, "Proportion of Case Dispositions by Case Type," in Paula Hannaford-Agor, Scott Graves, and Shelley Spacek Miller, *The Landscape of Civil Litigation in State Courts*, National Center for State Courts, 2015, p. 22). In some jurisdictions, the likelihood of a tort trial is even less. Only about 1.1 percent of all tort case dispositions in Florida circuit courts during fiscal year 2018–2019, for example, involved a jury or bench trial (Florida Office of the State Courts Administrator, "Circuit Civil Overview," in *FY 2018–19 Statistical Reference Guide*, March 2020, p. 4-22).

[13] Langton and Cohen (2008, p. 4) reports that 52 percent of tort trials in general jurisdiction court were decided in favor of the plaintiffs.

support. To the extent that such representation is obtained through the use of contingency fee agreements, these cases would have been judged by experienced counsel to have a high likelihood of a successful outcome and an expected compensation (used to calculate the fee) that would exceed the expected risk of no recovery and the law firm having to absorb any legal expenses advanced on the plaintiff's behalf. This type of vetting would filter out tort claims that are of only modest value or that have obvious problems with either the applicable law or their ability to prove necessary factual assertions.

Cases reaching the trial stage would certainly not be typical of tort litigation generally either. These cases are likely to have experienced defendant efforts to seek a pre-trial dispositive judgment in their favor, and indeed, about 40 percent of state court tort cases are either dismissed or end in a summary judgment.[14] The cases that survive that process would be perceived as potentially more valuable to the plaintiffs and potentially more costly to the defendants than most liability claims. The level of time and expense that plaintiffs' counsel would need to invest in the case ramps up considerably as the scheduled trial date approaches, so cases of relatively modest value may be increasingly seen as attractive candidates for more-certain settlement. Ultimately, the cases that both survive pre-trial efforts to dismiss and are perceived to be worthy enough to proceed to the first day of trial (despite the considerable costs for witnesses, forensic testing, investigation, and other trial-related expenses) at least have the potential for an award that is much larger than the average claim, as well as larger than the average value of claims that had been filed as lawsuits. Therefore, trial awards can have a disproportional impact on an insurer's overall liability compensation payments, even though the frequency of such awards would be dwarfed by the far larger universe of all tort claims received by the company on behalf of its insureds.[15]

---

[14] Hannaford-Agor, Graves, and Miller, 2015, Table 5.

[15] Insurer information on average tort claim payments and frequency, depending on whether the matter resulted in litigation or whether the litigation resulted in a trial award, is difficult for outsiders to acquire, but data from a now-discontinued closed claim database maintained by the Texas Department of Insurance (TDI) are instructive. Insurers were required to file reports with TDI on all claims closed under policies with general liability, medical professional liability, other professional liability, commercial automobile liability, or the liability portion of commercial multi-peril coverage. TDI's annual report for 2012 indicated that of such claims, 40 percent were closed without an associated lawsuit filing and resulted in payments that represented 25 percent of all compensation. The claims that did involve a lawsuit but were closed without having reached a verdict constituted 59 percent of the total count but 72 percent of total payments (this includes cases that went to trial but did not result in a verdict). Lawsuits that did result in a verdict were 1 percent of all claims but 3 percent of all payments. A rough approximation of relative value here suggests that verdict awards were three times the average claim payment (3 percent of total payments divided by 1 percent of total claims), the average payment for litigated claims was 22 percent greater than the overall average (72 percent divided by 59 percent), and the average payment for non-litigated claims was 37.5 percent less than the overall average (25 percent divided by 40 percent). It should be noted that reports to TDI were only required for claims payments of at least $25,000 in value. Unreported claims valued at less than $25,000 would have added to both the total count and the total payments in the breakout by resolution type discussed above had they been part of the TDI data collection. Assuming that the majority of such unreported claims were ones in which no lawsuit was filed, inclusion of these claims would have only enhanced the relative differences between average claim payments

But another potentially important impact of trial verdicts on the civil justice system is an indirect one. Information about recent verdicts in a particular jurisdiction or subject area has long been believed to cast a long and influential shadow over settlement negotiations in similar cases and, according to some observers, over other critical aspects of the entire civil dispute resolution mechanism as well, including an attorney's decision to accept a new client's case in the first place.[16]

Verdict Data

For this project, we turned to ALM (formerly known as American Lawyer Media), which provides specialized business news and information focused primarily on the legal, insurance, and commercial real estate sectors.[17] ALM's Law.com VerdictSearch unit is a leading provider of verdict reports, having acquired many major state and regional publications (referred to as "verdict reporters") that had been collecting and circulating information about verdicts for years. Typically, these reporting services rely on verdict summary forms (sometimes referred to as "case data questionnaires") voluntarily submitted by trial attorneys within a verdict reporter's geographical or jurisdictional coverage area.[18] The forms often collect information about

- the case caption
- the names of the parties and their attorneys
- the outcome of the case in terms of liability
- the total award (if any) granted to the plaintiffs
- the breakdown of the award by plaintiff, defendant, and damage type (if so structured)
- the underlying facts of the case (described in one or more paragraphs), as well as key allegations and defenses and the losses, damages, or injuries claimed by the plaintiffs.

The forms typically allow free text entry rather than selecting among predetermined choices, which potentially allows for a richer description of the case, although the reported information can then be less structured or lack consistency in details provided. Some forms also ask about the identity of expert witnesses testifying at a trial, the amounts asked of the trier of fact, the ages and occupations of the plaintiffs, and other details about the trial. When forms are submitted by attorneys for both the plaintiffs and the defendants, the reporters will

---

and those that either were litigated without verdict or did indeed reach a verdict (TDI, *The 2012 Texas Liability Insurance Closed Claim Annual Report*, 2014, Figure 21).

[16] See, for example, Stephen Daniels and Joanne Martin, *Civil Juries and the Politics of Reform*, Northwestern University Press, August 1995, p. 126; and Marc Galanter, "The Regulatory Function of the Civil Jury," in Robert E. Litan, ed., *Verdict: Assessing the Civil Jury System*, Brookings Institution Press, 1993, Chapter 3.

[17] ALM, homepage, undated-a.

[18] Verdict outcomes are not systematically reported in any detail by the courts in which the cases are filed.

seek to reconcile what was reported, sometimes by examining key court documents, such as the verdict form.

No verdict reporting service attempting to provide this rich level of detail about case outcomes can claim to have 100-percent coverage across metropolitan areas or regions. Although it might be possible to identify the cases that have concluded with a trial verdict within a specific geographical or jurisdictional area by examining information made available to the public by the local courts, the best complete sources for understanding what was asserted by the parties at trial are those who were actually present during the proceedings. Because it would not be possible to require such individuals to submit trial questionnaires to a for-profit enterprise, such as a verdict reporting service, the information has to be collected on a voluntary basis, and as a result, information gaps are inevitable. Later in this section, we discuss the implications of any shortfalls in the case data that are included in verdict reporting services' publications or databases.

Moreover, there is no verdict reporting service that can realistically claim national coverage. The absorption of individual reporters that once served metropolitan areas, regions, and states into larger corporate entities over the past three decades has resulted in more consistent reporting, but none has a national footprint. VerdictSearch acknowledges that its reporters are not uniformly distributed throughout the United States and that its coverage is concentrated on trials in the states of California, Georgia, Illinois, Florida, Michigan, New Jersey, New York, Ohio, Pennsylvania, and Texas, as well as regional coverage from the Carolinas, the D.C. metropolitan area, and New England.[19] The states where coverage is focused clearly skew toward some of the most populous and most urbanized in the country, but we are unaware of any claims that social inflation is an issue primarily encountered in more rural locations. Thus, if there are observable trends in awards that suggest a social inflation effect, they should be present in the VerdictSearch data.

We purchased ten years' worth of verdict outcomes from VerdictSearch, covering verdicts reached between 2010 and 2019. We chose this ten-year window because we believed that VerdictSearch's ability to gather verdict information would have been relatively stable during this period and because it was a time when the topic of social inflation was repeatedly discussed in insurance industry publications. Ending the analysis in 2019 also avoided possible issues related to the impacts of the COVID-19 pandemic.

Information related to 41,590 case outcomes was included in the VerdictSearch data that we acquired, but focusing only on reports related to trial verdicts during the ten-year period reduced our analysis dataset to 37,668 cases. An important initial task was to organize the verdicts by subject matter. Our primary interest was to analyze cases in which personal injury or wrongful death (PI/WD) tort liability was at issue, which are the types of cases that arguably receive the most attention from those who believe social inflation has become a disruptive influence in the civil justice system in general and in the insurance industry in particular. Because VerdictSearch's classification system for trial reports does not explicitly indicate

[19] ALM, "Law.com VerdictSearch: Featured Verdicts," webpage, undated-b.

whether any tort-based legal theory was involved, we first searched for cases in which allegations of physical or mental injuries (both fatal and non-fatal) were present, which are the type of claims that were very likely to require proof of liability based on tort law principles. Once such cases were identified, we then examined information in each report for terms that suggested tort liability was at least one of the legal theories on which the claim was brought. Verdicts meeting both the claimed injuries test and the tort terms test would then be classified as PI/WD tort cases for the purposes of our analysis.

The VerdictSearch data have an open-ended "injury_text" field for each plaintiff in a report, but its purpose is for providing a detailed description of the losses claimed by a plaintiff for any type of harm, which could refer to contractual or business-related financial losses rather than those rising from personal injuries or death (e.g., medical expenses, wage loss, pain and suffering, loss of support).[20] But our analysis of three other plaintiff-specific fields for "injury_name" suggested that, except for instances in which the fields were used only for recording the sex and age of the plaintiff, non-blank values consistently described physical or mental injuries, including those that resulted in death.[21] As a result of that review, we used those fields to indicate whether each plaintiff in one of our verdict reports had brought claims of non-fatal physical and\or mental injuries or claims involving wrongful death.[22] Plaintiff-level descriptions that were not flagged as involving personal injuries or wrongful death were deemed to have only made claims for other types of losses or damages, such as business interruption expenses or lost profits.

After identifying the broad category of losses for each plaintiff, we made case-level classifications of loss type based on a simple rule: Instances in which there were any WD allegations advanced by any plaintiff would result in the entire case being identified as a WD action, cases without WD allegations but in which at least one plaintiff sought damages related to personal injuries would be designated as a PI case, and all other cases would be classified as seeking non-PI/WD type losses.

Our next step was to examine VerdictSearch "case_type" fields in PI/WD verdicts for terms that were consistent with common tort-related fact patterns, such as "assault," "dog bite," "dram shop," "electrocution," "harassment," or "motor vehicle." Thus, the cases that we used for our analysis were chosen because they both involved claims of personal injuries or wrongful death and had been labeled by VerdictSearch with tags that suggested the case might involve theories of negligence, products liability, or intentional harm.

It should be noted that our approach for identifying PI/WD tort cases would exclude otherwise legitimate tort cases in which the only losses being claimed were for property damage. However, we believe that litigation reaching the trial stage in a general jurisdiction state trial court (rather than in a small claims setting) that involves property losses as the sole damage

---

[20] The "injury_text" field often contains multiple paragraphs of text.

[21] The "injury_name" field characterizes injuries using a taxonomy developed by ALM.

[22] Verdicts that were identified as involving physical or mental injuries but also had the word "death" in the "injury_text" field were treated as arising from WD claims.

claimed would be relatively uncommon. Our approach also excludes *hybrid* cases from being identified as a tort case. These business, contract, real property, or equity disputes involve tort-like aspects that broaden the possible damages available, such as a case alleging an insurer's bad-faith denial of a homeowner's fire damage claim, which could lead to a punitive damage award. Social inflation could have considerable impact on these hybrid cases.

Using this approach to identify verdicts in PI/WD tort cases between 2010 and 2019 reduced the number of VerdictSearch cases in our sample to 26,115. We then excluded one case from the sample that resulted in a $150 billion verdict (which is more than six times the size of the next largest plaintiff award in our dataset). We viewed that case, the largest non-class action tort verdict in U.S. history at the time, as an extreme outlier that provided little, if any, information about trends in jury verdicts.[23]

Cases from all 50 states, the District of Columbia, Puerto Rico, and the Virgin Islands are included in the VerdictSearch data. Texas, New York, California, Pennsylvania, Florida, Illinois, and New Jersey (in order of number of cases) account for 82 percent of the total (see Table 3.5). The number of verdicts ranged from 1,128 to 1,926 per year. The vast majority of the verdicts (96 percent) occur in state court, and class actions and other multiple-plaintiff verdicts are uncommon. The number of plaintiffs in verdicts with awards ranged from 1 to 36: 70 percent of verdicts with awards had only one plaintiff, and 22 percent had two. The number of plaintiffs was between three and five for an additional 7 percent of plaintiff wins. Only 1 percent had more than five plaintiffs.

Once we had identified PI/WD cases, the task of categorizing the underlying fact patterns was more straightforward. A first step was to classify defendants by whether they appeared to be sued as a business, a government agency, a nonprofit, or another type of organization. VerdictSearch includes a "company" flag in its database to indicate whether a named defendant is a business, but the value is missing for slightly more than one-third of all defendants. In addition, examination of defendant names for those that had been flagged as non-business suggested a considerable percentage of false negatives. In order to fill that gap, we performed an analysis of the defendant name fields that lacked an existing determination of company status in the data. Starting with keywords in a set of names of defendants that were obviously organizational, we applied those words to the remainder of the name strings, performed an eyes-on review of both positive and negative hits, and refined the search terms before repeating the process. We eventually developed a list of more than 700 target words, such as "Academy," "Council," "Corp.," "Fitness," "Housing," "Motors," "Partners," "Refining," "Southeastern," "Vascular," and "World," as search strings. That list also contained entries that would help identify instances in which an individual defendant was being sued in an official or business capacity, such as "Doctor," "Sheriff," "Esq," "M.D.," "Official Capacity," or "Sgt." Ultimately, we designated a case as one involving organizational defendants if any defendant

[23] As described in the ALM database, both the victim and perpetrator were minors at the time of the 1998 incident, and the case involved sexual assault and wrongful death. In 2011, a Texas jury awarded $150 billion in punitive damages and $370 million in compensatory damages.

TABLE 3.5

PI/WD Tort Verdicts Between 2010 and 2019 Included in This Analysis

Verdict Subset	Number of Verdicts	Percentage of Verdicts	Plaintiff Win Rate (%)	Number of Trial Awards
All verdicts	26,114	100.0	57.5	15,017
Case type				
Medical malpractice	2,553	9.8	34.8	888
Commercial trucking	1,068	4.1	64.0	683
Other commercial vehicles	3,234	12.4	69.1	2,235
Private auto	9,913	38.0	64.6	6,405
Other cases against organizational defendants	8,071	30.9	51.6	4,165
Other cases against non-organizational defendants	1,275	4.9	50.3	641
Claimed harm				
Bodily injury	23,872	91.4	57.8	13,808
Wrongful death	2,242	8.6	53.9	1,209
Brain injury indication				
Serious brain injury	2,170	8.3	59.4	1,288
Other brain injury	5,946	22.8	61.2	3,637
No brain injury	17,998	68.9	56.1	10,092
State				
California	3,628	13.9	55.5	2,013
Florida	2,379	9.1	61.6	1,465
Illinois	1,496	5.7	57.4	859
New Jersey	1,484	5.7	60.8	902
New York	4,707	18.0	52.1	2,451
Pennsylvania	2,413	9.2	47.9	1,156
Texas	5,205	19.9	60.9	3,171
All other states	4,802	18.4	62.5	3,000

SOURCE: Authors' analysis of 2010–2019 VerdictSearch data.

in that case either had been flagged by VerdictSearch as a business or had a positive result when the defendant's name was searched using our target words.

Our analysis of the database's "case_type" fields, as well as its detailed free text "facts" fields, concluded that in the PI/WD tort cases that we had identified, certain keywords in these fields could group the cases by whether they involved medical malpractice allegations or motor vehicle collisions and other road-related incidents. Other types of PI/WD torts, such as cases related to product-caused injuries, falls caused by slippery surfaces, animal bites, and the like were simply included in an "other tort" category because we could not reliably identify the specific type of underlying incident with our text string search strategy.

Identification of organizational defendants was especially important in cases that we had flagged as motor vehicle torts because doing so allowed us to distinguish the large pool of actions that sought to recover damages from individuals with private passenger vehicle policies from those seeking compensation from businesses and other entities. A subset of the commercial (i.e., organizational defendant) motor vehicle tort cases was later identified as involving trucks or other large vehicles using keyword searches of the free text fact descriptions, with such terms as "bobtail truck," "tank trailer," or "18-wheeler." Some have argued that social inflation affects organizational defendants to a greater degree than non-organizational defendants, and to facilitate investigation of this hypothesis, we split verdicts in the "other tort" category into those against organizational defendants and those against non-organizational defendants. The number of verdicts in each of the resulting six case type categories is shown in Table 3.5.

Using VerdictSearch data also allowed us to classify verdicts by claimed medical consequence. Slightly less than 9 percent of the verdicts involved wrongful death, and the remainder involved non-fatal physical injury (see Table 3.5). Emotional injuries also may have been alleged in these cases. One area of interest involves non-fatal traumatic brain injuries, a type of loss said to "increase the risk of [a claim] outcome significantly influenced by Social Inflation."[24] To identify allegations of harm to the brain or any impact on cognitive functions, we examined the descriptions of the claimed injuries. We searched the injury description fields for such terms as "brain," "cerebral palsy," "concussion," "hemicraniectomy," "stroke," or "unconsciousness" to flag any potential neurological issue, then used a subset of those terms, including "encephalomalacia," "hydrocephalus," and "subarachnoid hemorrhage," as evidence that a potentially more serious injury had been alleged. As shown in Table 3.5, approximately 8 percent of PI/WD tort cases that went to verdict appeared to involve more serious brain injuries, while 23 percent had evidence of a brain injury that could not be identified by our text string searches as relatively more serious.

Lawsuit Frequency Data

Our analysis of trends in the frequency of tort lawsuits relied on data from the National Center for State Courts (NCSC). We used data from the 19 states that have tracked net tort filings in their general jurisdiction courts for at least a decade in a manner consistent with NCSC standards for reporting caseloads.[25] These data were augmented with filing counts from the California Judicial Council (California was not one of the 19 states).

[24] Michael Bruton, "Identify Factors Contributing to Social Inflation," *DocLens.ai Blogs*, October 18, 2022.

[25] Cases that removed to federal court would still be included in the state court filing numbers.

Price Inflation Adjustments

As indicated at the outset of this report, a core claim about social inflation is that the expansion of liability causes the compensation paid for different types of tort claims to grow faster than what would be expected given ordinary price inflation. Therefore, any observed trends in tort claims or tort trial awards need to be considered in light of what we know about the rise in the overall costs of goods and services in the U.S. economy over the ten-year study period (2010–2019). The discussion that follows describes how we accounted for price inflation in analyzing claim severity and trial awards.

Adjustments for Trial Awards

We adjust plaintiffs' monetary awards in our verdict data using the U.S. Bureau of Economic Analysis' personal consumption expenditures price index (PCEPI), which is the Federal Reserve's preferred measure of the prices that people living in the United States (or those buying on their behalf) pay for goods and services. When setting the award in a PI case, jurors consider such damages as wage loss, medical treatment costs, and long-term care costs, as well as noneconomic damages, such as pain and suffering and punitive damages. In WD cases, the focus of setting an award is usually on determining the financial support that the deceased would have provided to survivors but for death. Different inflation adjustments might be appropriate for various components. For example, medical costs might reasonably be adjusted by a medical care price index. However, VerdictSearch does not provide consistent information on how awards break down along these lines, in part because juries may not provide any such information. We thus use the general PCEPI to adjust for inflation, which includes a medical cost component (see Figure 3.1).[26]

Adjustments for Insurance Claims Severity and Loss Ratios

We are interested in the growth of insurance claim costs in excess of the general rate of inflation, and thus, we adjust severity using an appropriate inflation index. In our analysis of insurance claims, we examined BI and PD claims.

---

[26] The PCEPI uses the component indices of the Consumer Price Index (CPI) as inputs (see Wesley Janson, Randal Verbrugge, and Carola Conces Binder, "The CPI-PCEPI Inflation Differential: Causes and Prospects," *Economic Commentary*, Federal Reserve Bank of Cleveland, Number 2020-06, March 2, 2020). The CPI adjusts some components for quality (putting downward pressure on the price index when quality improves), and thus, it may not capture the full increase in the cost of replacement parts or services when quality improves. Such an effect would tend to cause our analysis to overstate social inflation. However, only roughly 15 percent of 273 CPI "entry level items (ELIs)" are adjusted for quality, and the ELIs of particular interest in this study are not adjusted for quality. Specifically, these unadjusted ELIs are as follows: physical services, hospital services, nursing and convalescent care, drugs, vehicle parts and equipment, vehicle repair, vehicle maintenance and servicing, and motor vehicle body work (U.S. Bureau of Labor Statistics, "Consumer Price Index: Quality Adjustment in the CPI," webpage, March 12, 2024).

FIGURE 3.1
Price Indices Used to Construct Inflation Adjustments

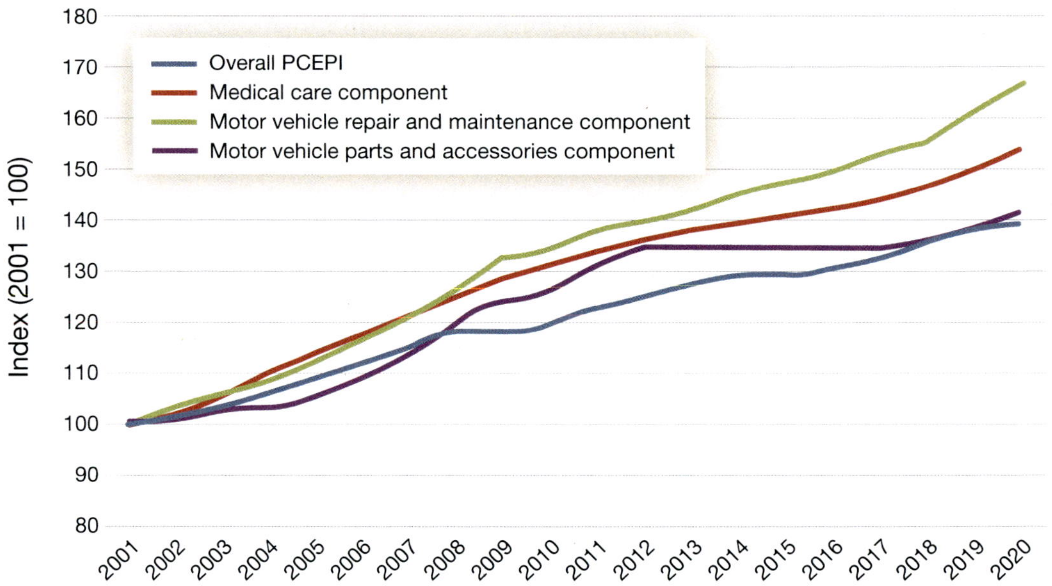

SOURCE: Authors' analysis using data from Federal Reserve Bank of St. Louis, "Table 2.4.4. Price Indexes for Personal Consumption Expenditures by Type of Product: Annual," FRED release, undated.

Payments for BI claims can contain components for medical care, lost wages, and pain and suffering. Thus, we adjusted the severity of BI claims using a weighted sum of the inflation rates of the overall PCEPI and the PCEPI medical care component. Relying on Verisk's experience with claims data, we placed one-half of the weight on the PCEPI and one-half on the medical care component of the PCEPI. Between 2001 and 2019, the medical care component of the PCEPI grew more rapidly than the overall PCEPI (see Figure 3.1).

The PCEPI is used to adjust severity for PD claims that do not apply to a particular economic sector.[27] For example, the PCEPI is used to adjust severity for first-party commercial property claims. The motor vehicle parts and accessories and the motor vehicle repair and maintenance components of the PCEPI are used to adjust PD claims for commercial and personal automobile claims. For motor vehicle PD claims, we used a weighted sum of the above motor vehicle components and refer to the result as the *motor vehicle PD price index*. The weights (two-thirds for maintenance and repair and one-third for parts and equipment) were chosen to reflect the relative weight of these two components in the PCEPI.

Figure 3.2 shows the year-over-year changes in the price indices used to adjust the severity of BI claims (*BI price index*) for economic inflation and the two price indices that were used

[27] See Federal Reserve Bank of St. Louis, undated.

FIGURE 3.2

Year-Over-Year Percentage Change in the Price Indices Used to Adjust Claim Severity for Economic Inflation

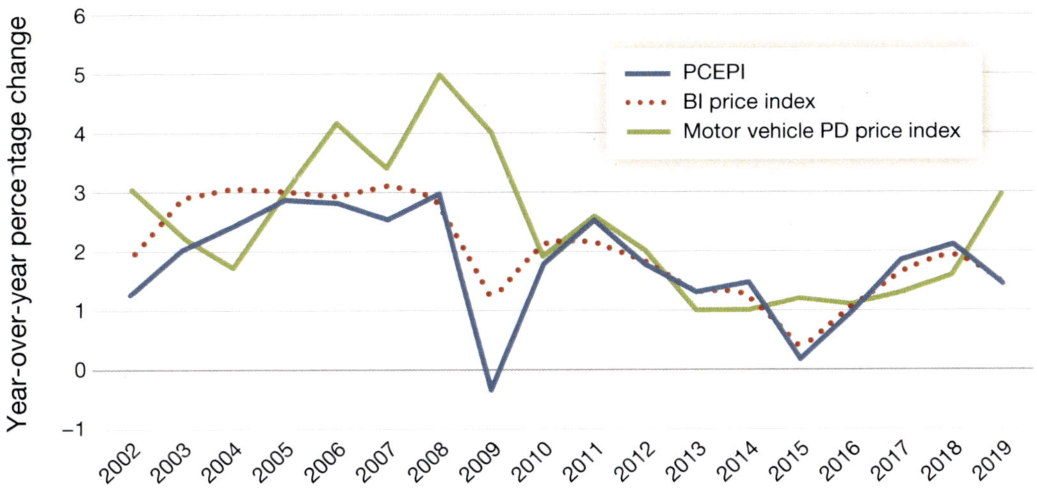

SOURCE: Authors' analysis using data from Federal Reserve Bank of St. Louis, undated.

to adjust PD claims (the PCEPI and the motor vehicle PD price index). Except for the second half of the 2000s, changes in the three price indices were similar. Following the onset of the Great Recession, the growth rate in the PCEPI declined, while that for the motor vehicle PD index remained high. Table 3.6 reports the annual percentage change in the three indices over various periods.

As a price index, the PCEPI medical care component does not directly consider changes in the amount of health care consumed.[28] Increases in the amount of health care consumed

TABLE 3.6

Average Annual Growth Rates for Price Indices Used in This Study

	Annual Growth Rate (%)		
Period	PCEPI	BI Price Index	Motor Vehicle PD Price Index
2001–2010	2.1	2.6	3.2
2011–2019	1.5	1.5	1.7
2001–2019	1.8	2.0	2.4

SOURCE: Authors' analysis using data from Federal Reserve Bank of St. Louis, undated.

28 The PCEPI would pick up changes in the mix of health care goods and services of consumed, which would likely change as the quantity of goods and services changes.

could be due to changes in medical treatment and health care practices, both of which could lead to increases in trial awards and insurance claim severity absent social inflation. We investigated the sensitivity of our results under various assumptions regarding changes in medical treatment and health care practices. Our approach is described in Appendix A.

CHAPTER 4

Litigation Trends

Although we primarily focus on insurance tort claims and tort trial awards, it is useful to examine possible social inflationary effects on the propensity to initiate tort litigation. One claim (discussed in Chapter 2) is that social inflation is driving up the frequency of tort lawsuits generally, so examining data on court filings from multiple jurisdictions could be instructive. A second assertion is that social inflation might be expected to push up the plaintiff win rate at trial. In this chapter, we provide some initial data relative to these hypotheses. We also examine trends in the percentage of filings that go to trial. Changes in the number of filings that go to trial are relevant to interpreting the trial awards reported in the following chapter. A reduction could indicate that increasingly only the higher-stakes cases are going to verdict (which could be another possible explanation for a rise in the size of trial awards).

Case Filings

Despite the fact that the basic legal concepts related to tort litigation are similar in every state and tort cases constitute a sizeable proportion of all state court civil lawsuits, only a subset of states have tracked tort filings in their general jurisdiction courts for at least a decade in a manner consistent with NCSC standards for reporting caseloads.[1] Using data from only those 19 states, Figure 4.1 shows that the annual number of new tort case filings per capita rose about 10 percent between 2012 and 2019.[2] The tort case filing rate oscillates up and down during the first part of this period but then steadily increases in the second half of the 2010s. In contrast, total civil case filings per capita fell by about 10 percent over this period.

California data were not included in the analysis for Figure 4.1, but data from California provide additional insight into tort litigation trends in the United States. Tort litigation comprises a much larger percentage of all civil litigation in California than in the 19 states

[1] The following 19 states track tort filings consistent with NCSC guidelines: Alaska, Colorado, Connecticut, Florida, Hawaii, Indiana, Kentucky, Maryland, Michigan, Nevada, New Hampshire, New Jersey, New York, North Dakota, Ohio, Pennsylvania, South Carolina, Texas, and Utah.

[2] Tort case filings in these 19 states rose about 16 percent between 2012 and 2019, and the U.S. population rose about 5 percent (U.S. Census Bureau, "State Population Totals and Components of Change: 2010–2019," webpage, November 4, 2021).

FIGURE 4.1
Civil and Tort Case Filings per Capita in 19 States

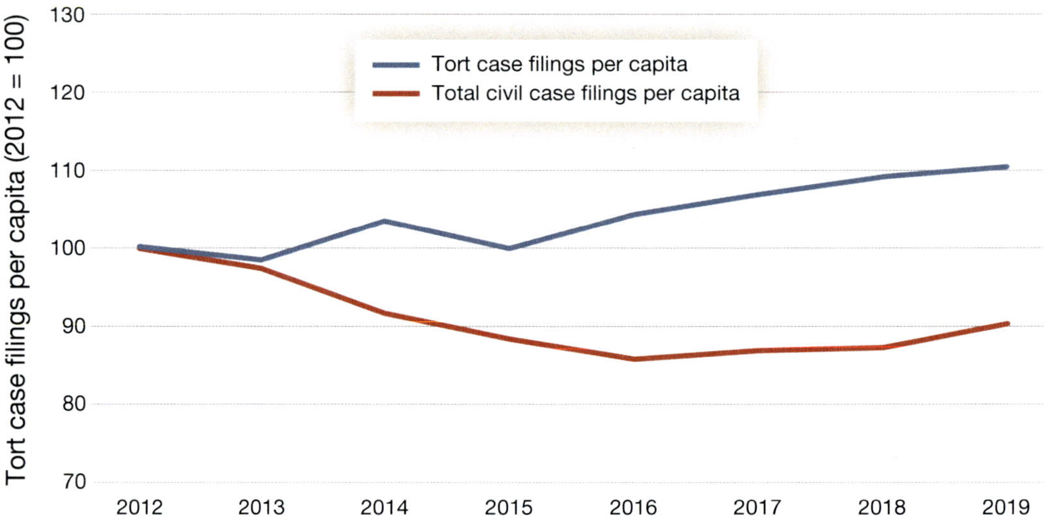

SOURCE: Authors' analysis using 2012–2019 data from S. Gibson, B. Harris, N. Waters, K. Genthon, M. Hamilton, E. Bailey Stevens, M. Moffett, and D. Robinson, eds., "CSP STAT Civil," Court Statistics Project database, National Center for State Courts and Conference of State Court Administrators, October 9, 2023.

examined, and that percentage has been growing (30 percent in 2020 versus 23 percent in 2011). As Figure 4.2 indicates, there has been a very notable surge in motor vehicle tort case filings per capita over a recent nine-year period: The 2019 filing rate reflects an approximate 40-percent increase over the 2011 filing rate. Filing of non-motor vehicle torts per capita remained roughly flat over this period, with the result that total tort case filings per capita increased by slightly more than 20 percent.

The spike in motor vehicle tort cases in California without a parallel increase in other types of tort claims suggests that the cause is specific to these types of claims. Data from the California Highway Patrol covering 2010–2019 show noticeable bumps in both fatal and non-fatal accidents (Figure 4.3). Whatever the reason, tort litigation in California appears to have increased during the second decade of the 21st century.

Verdicts per Case Filed

As shown in Figure 4.4, the number of tort case filings in the 19 states for which consistent data are available rose from 2014 to 2019, while the number of PI/WD verdicts in the VerdictSearch database for the same 19 states declined during this period. Because verdicts only occur sometime after cases are filed, the figure shows the number of case filings two years prior to the year in which the verdicts were reached. Thus, for 2014, Figure 4.4 shows the number of verdicts in 2014 and the number of cases filed in 2012 at the same point on the horizontal axis. The con-

FIGURE 4.2
Tort Case Filings per Capita in California, 2011–2019

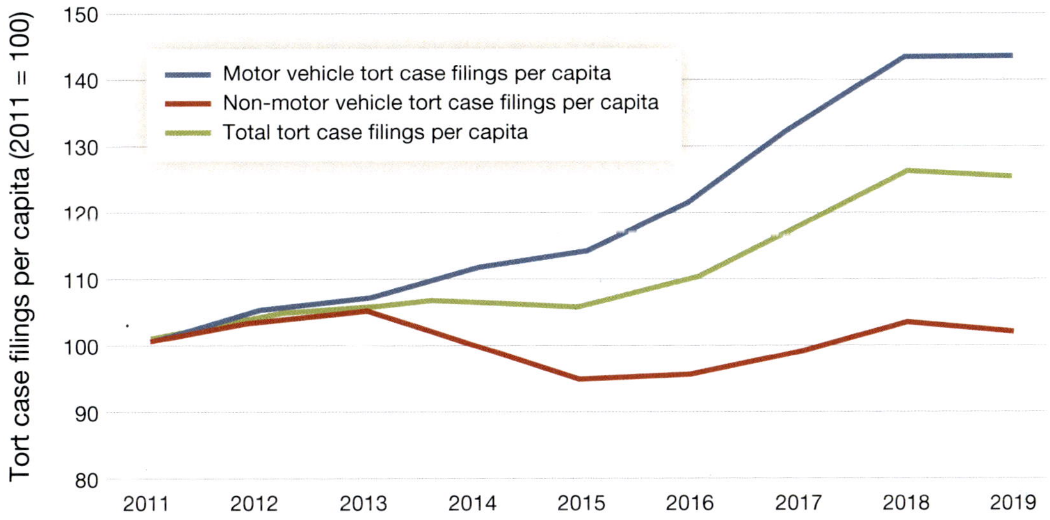

SOURCE: Authors' analysis using data from Judicial Council of California, *2021 Court Statistics Report: Statewide Caseload Trends, 2010–11 Through 2019–20*, 2021, p. 79, and U.S. Census Bureau, 2021.

FIGURE 4.3
Fatal and Non-Fatal Injury Motor Vehicle Crashes per Capita in California

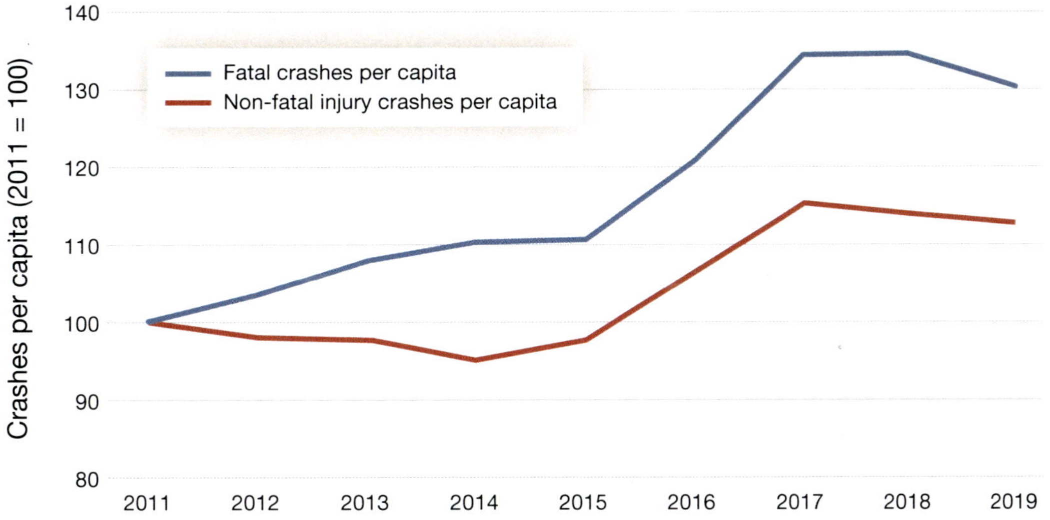

SOURCE: Features information from California Highway Patrol, "SWITRS 2019 Report: 2019 Annual Report of Fatal and Injury Motor Vehicle Traffic Crashes," webpage, undated.

FIGURE 4.4

Comparison of Tort Cases Filed and Tort Verdicts in VerdictSearch Database in 19 States

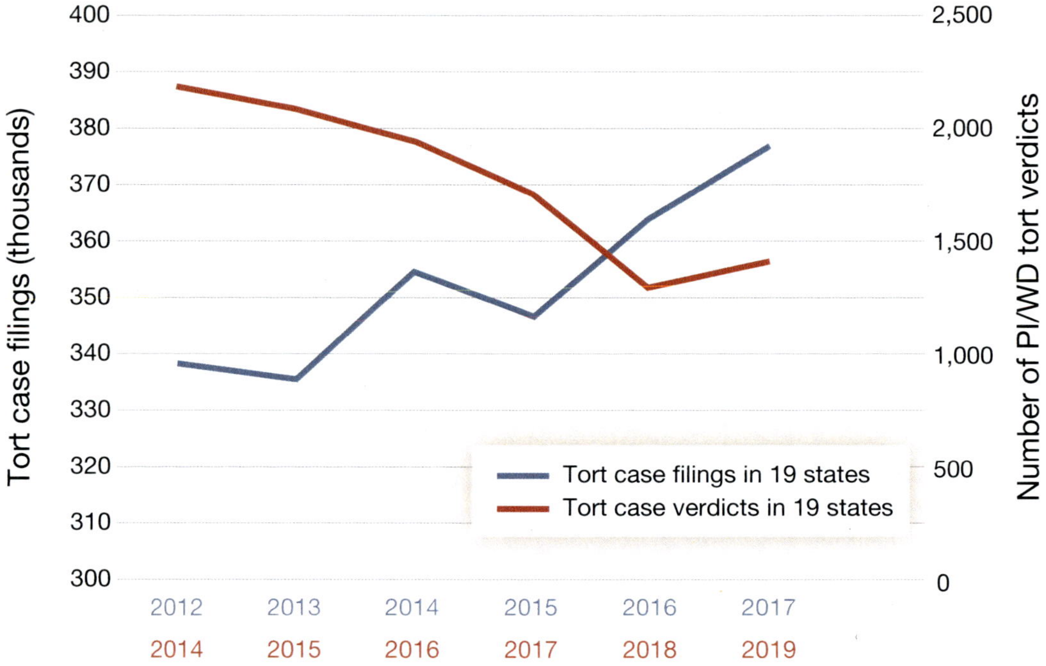

SOURCE: Authors' analysis using data from Gibson et al., 2023 (cases filed), and VerdictSearch data (PI/WD tort case verdicts).

NOTE: Because verdicts only occur sometime after cases are filed, the figure shows the number of case filings two years prior (year $t - 2$) to the year (year t) in which the verdicts were reached.

sequence of these two trends is that the ratio of verdicts in the VerdictSearch database to the number of cases filed two years previously nearly halved between 2014 and 2019 (see Figure 4.5). This change could be due to a drop in the percentage of cases that reached trial, a drop in the percentage of trials that reached a verdict, a decline in the percentage of verdicts reported to VerdictSearch, or some combination of these possibilities.

Plaintiff Win Rate

The percentage of reported PI/WD tort verdicts in our dataset that resulted in a monetary award for the plaintiff rose considerably over the study period. We refer to this as the *plaintiff win rate*, although this rate would include awards that are less than the settlement amount offered by the defendant or their insurers. Such awards might be viewed as wins for the defendants or their insurers. For the 26,114 verdicts in the study dataset, the plaintiff win rate rose from 52 percent in 2010 to 64 percent in 2019 (see Figure 4.6). The plaintiff win rate at the

FIGURE 4.5
PI/WD Tort Verdicts in VerdictSearch Database as a Percentage of Cases Filed Two Years Earlier in 19 States

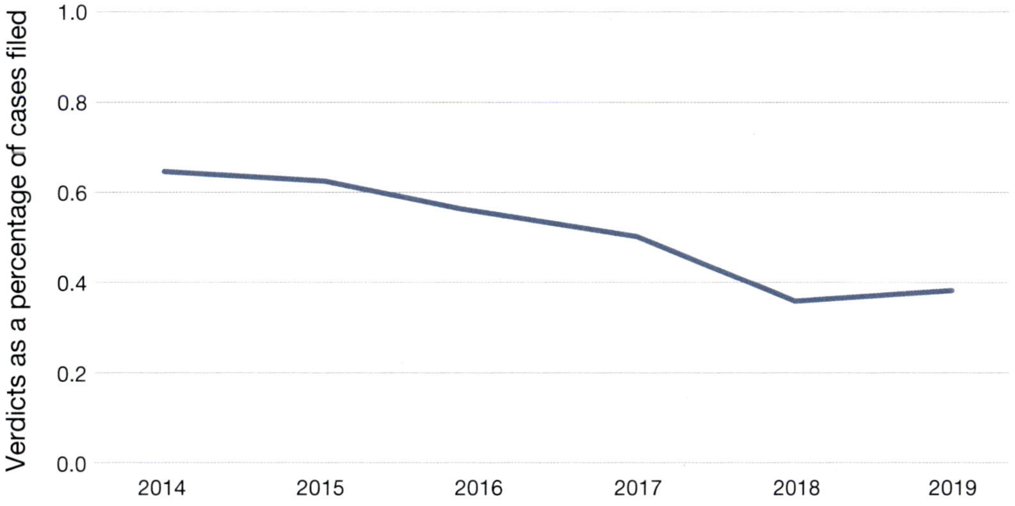

SOURCE: Authors' analysis using data from Gibson et al., 2023 (cases filed), and VerdictSearch data (PI/WD tort verdicts).

NOTE: Because verdicts only occur sometime after cases are filed, in this figure, verdicts in a given year (year *t*) correspond to the number of case filings two years prior (year *t* – 2).

FIGURE 4.6
Plaintiff Win Rate for All PI/WD Tort Verdicts in Dataset

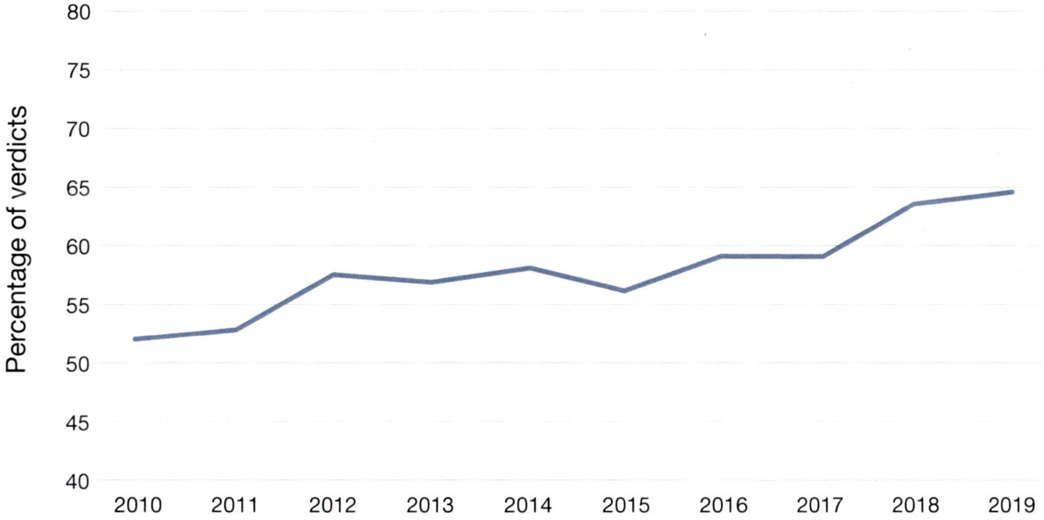

SOURCE: Features information from 2010–2019 VerdictSearch data.

NOTE: N = 26,114 verdicts.

beginning of the period matches that reported in a 2005 census of verdicts in a set of jurisdictions.[3] The consistency of the two findings provides some reassurance that the cases in the VerdictSearch database are broadly representative of all PI/WD tort verdicts, at least at the beginning of the period.

The plaintiff win rate reported in Figure 4.6 does not factor in changes over the study period in case type distribution, the state in which the case was brought, or the type of harm claimed. Using the statistical approach described in Appendix A, we projected the plaintiff win rate controlling for these factors. As shown in Figure 4.7, the results are quite similar to those in Figure 4.6. Figure 4.8 shows the change in plaintiff win rate from year to year using the same statistical approach. As can be seen, the win rate rose by over three percentage points multiple times during the study period, and there is no strong evidence that the win rate rose more rapidly in the second half of the period than in the first half.

The plaintiff win rate varies by case type, and we examined how it changed for various case types. As shown in Table 4.1, the plaintiff win rate between 2010 and 2019 ranged from a low of 34.8 percent for medical malpractice cases to a high of 69.1 percent in commercial motor vehicle cases not involving trucks, tractors, and trailers.

We found that the plaintiff win rate rose during our study period for many types of cases. Table 4.2 shows the annual percentage point increase in the win rate that best fits the changes

FIGURE 4.7

Estimated Plaintiff Win Rate, Controlling for Changes in Case Characteristics

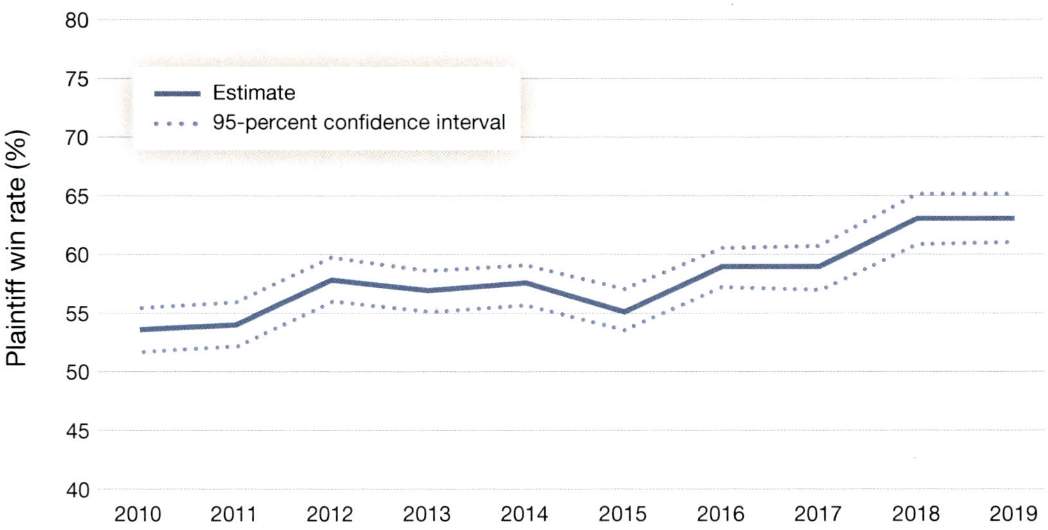

SOURCE: Authors' analysis using 2010–2019 VerdictSearch data.

NOTE: Our analysis controlled for changes over the study period in case type distribution, the state in which the case was brought, and the type of harm claimed. N = 26,114 verdicts.

---

[3] See Table 5, "Percent of Plaintiff Winners in Civil Trials in State Courts, by Case Type, 2005," in Langton and Cohen, 2008.

FIGURE 4.8

Estimated Annual Percentage Point Change in Plaintiff Win Rate, Controlling for Case Characteristics

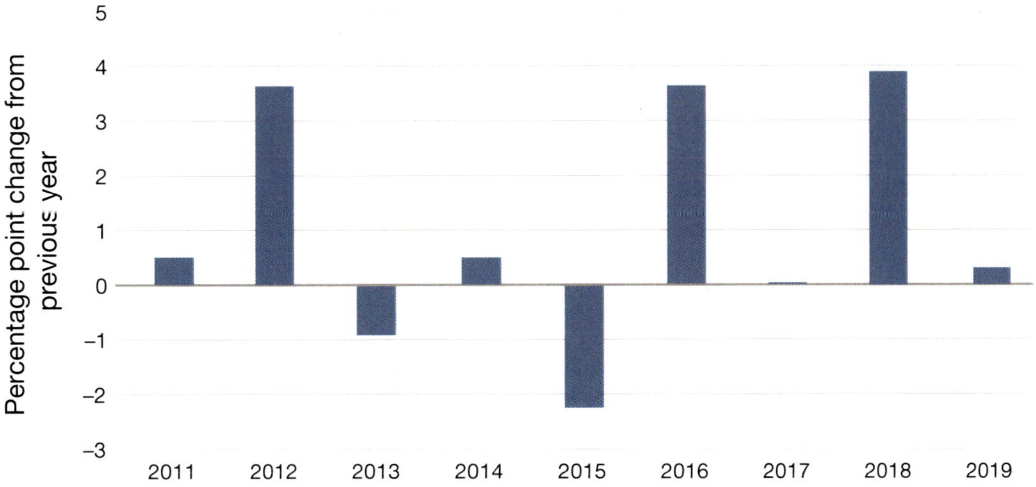

SOURCE: Authors' analysis using 2010–2019 VerdictSearch data.

NOTE: Our analysis controlled for changes over the study period in case type distribution, the state in which the case was brought, and the type of harm claimed. N = 26,114 verdicts.

TABLE 4.1

Plaintiff Win Rates in PI/WD Tort Verdicts, 2010–2019

Verdict Category	Number of Verdicts	Plaintiff Win Rate (%)
All verdicts	26,114	57.5
Case type		
Medical malpractice	2,553	34.8
Commercial trucking	1,068	64.0
Other commercial vehicles	3,234	69.1
Private auto	9,913	64.6
Other cases against organizational defendants	8,071	51.6
Other cases against non-organizational defendants	1,275	50.3

SOURCE: Authors' analysis of 2010–2019 VerdictSearch data.

TABLE 4.2
Growth in Plaintiff Win Rate from 2010 Through 2019, Controlling for Case Characteristics

Verdict Category	Growth (percentage points per year)
All verdicts	0.90***
Organizational defendants	
Commercial trucking	0.72
Other commercial vehicles	0.93***
Medical malpractice	0.16
Other cases against organizational defendants	1.33***
Non-organizational defendants	
Private auto	0.58***
Other cases against non-organizational defendants	2.19***

SOURCE: Authors' analysis of 2010–2019 VerdictSearch data.
NOTE: * = statistically different from 0 with 90-percent probability; ** = statistically different from 0 with 95-percent probability; *** = statistically different from 0 with 99-percent probability.
N = 26,114.

in win rate over the study period, controlling for case characteristics. For verdicts as a whole, the plaintiff win rate rose 0.90 of a percentage point per year over the study period. The win rate rose for all six case types examined, although the increase in the win rate for medical malpractice verdicts was small and not statistically different from zero. The increases for verdicts that fall into the "other" case type categories are particularly large—increasing 1.33 percentage points per year for organizational defendants and 2.19 percentage points per year for non-organizational defendants.

Discussion

As discussed in Chapter 2, an increase in the number of tort case filings brought against potential responsible parties is a hypothesized consequence of social inflation. The findings in this chapter provide evidence that tort case filings per capita increased during the study period. However, we do not know whether this increase was caused by factors associated with social inflation or other factors, such as an increase in underlying tortious incidents.[4] With its

4 Another potentially confounding factor is change in inflation-adjusted gross domestic product (GDP) per capita. The annual percentage change in annual real GDP per capita in the United States varied between 0.8 percent and 2.4 percent between 2010 and 2019. These increases followed a –0.8 percent change in 2008 and a –3.4 percent change in 2009. The steady increases between 2010 and 2019 do not suggest that changing economic activity was a significant factor in the change in tort case filing rates. (GDP growth rates are based

parallel rise in vehicle crash and tort case filing rates, California provides a potential example of the latter factor. Further work is needed to understand the factors that are pushing up case filings per capita, but their increase supports the contention that social inflation is occurring. The increase in the plaintiff win rate for verdicts in the VerdictSearch database is also consistent with anticipated effects of social inflation. One possible mechanism that could lead to such an increase is delayed defense response to changes in case values. If defendants are not making settlement offers that are keeping up with rising settlement values, cases that plaintiffs will win might go to trial that would have settled otherwise. Over time, defense strategy might adapt, and the plaintiff win rate could return to previous levels.

Other factors, however, could also be responsible for the observed increase in the number of tort case filings. For example, prior research suggests that defense verdicts, verdicts in which the plaintiffs received relatively modest awards, and verdicts without a punitive damage component are underrepresented in verdict reporter publications and databases, presumably because of the voluntary nature of the submissions.[5] Although defense verdicts may be underrepresented in VerdictSearch, the question relevant to interpreting the increase in the plaintiff win rate observed in our sample is whether, *relative to plaintiffs' attorneys*, defense attorneys became less likely to report defense verdicts over the study period. The lack of alignment between the relatively steady increase in plaintiff win rate and the bump up in the growth rate of trial awards later in the mid-2010s reported in this chapter also raise questions about whether the increase in plaintiff win rate could be due to social inflation. Further work is needed to understand whether and how verdict reporting rates have changed over time and any other factors that might be behind an increase in the plaintiff win rate.

Our finding that the ratio of verdicts in the VerdictSearch database to the number of cases filed in the NCSC data for 19 states declined has potential implications for how to interpret the findings on trial awards in the next chapter. For example, if court staffing has not kept up with the increase in the number of cases, larger caseloads could result in longer time to trial, which could result in litigants taking only higher-value cases to trial. A decline in the ratio of verdicts to cases could also be driven by a decreased likelihood that either defense or plaintiff

---

on our calculations using data on real GDP from U.S. Bureau of Economic Analysis, "Real Gross Domestic Product [GDPC1]," FRED database, Federal Reserve Bank of St. Louis, April 25, 2024; and U.S. population data from World Bank, "Population, Total for United States [POPTOTUSA647NWDB]," FRED database, Federal Reserve Bank of St. Louis, July 4, 2023.)

[5] See, for example, Nicholas M. Pace, Daniela Golinelli, and Laura Zakaras, *Capping Non-Economic Awards in Medical Malpractice Trials: California Jury Verdicts Under MICRA*, RAND Corporation, MG-234-ICJ, 2004, pp. 63–65. An attempt to compare the entries in jury verdict reporters with official court records concluded that the publications "recorded only half of the jury trials that took place," reported plaintiff win rates that were "9 percent higher," and were "systematically skewed towards higher compensatory and punitive awards" ("Verdict Reports Overstate Awards" in Paula Hannaford-Agor, Robert C. LaFountain, and Shauna Strickland, "Trial Trends and Implications for the Civil Justice System," *Caseload Highlights*, Vol. 11, No. 3, National Center for State Courts, June 2005, p. 3).

verdicts are reported to VerdictSearch.[6] A decline in the likelihood that defense verdicts are reported would not pose a problem for our analysis of the size of trial awards, but a decline in the likelihood that plaintiff verdicts are reported could mean that increasingly only larger trial awards are found in our data for the later years of the study period. Both an increase in court caseloads and a decline in the likelihood that plaintiff verdicts are reported could lead to an increase in the trial awards absent social inflation. Although such scenarios are plausible, further investigation is needed to establish the extent to which they have had an impact on trial awards.

[6] The plaintiff win rate rose by about 20 percent between 2014 and 2019, while the ratio of verdicts to cases filed two years earlier fell by about 40 percent. Thus, even if enough additional defense verdicts had been reported to keep the plaintiff win rate unchanged, roughly a 20-percent drop in the verdicts per filing would remain.

CHAPTER 5

Ten Years of Trial Awards

In this chapter, we present findings on trends in PI/WD tort trial awards between 2010 and 2019. We begin by examining trends in all PI/WD awards, then proceed to examine trends in awards by case type, claimed harm, and state. For each set of verdicts examined, we report the compound annual growth rate (CAGR) in inflation-adjusted awards per plaintiff between 2010 and 2019.[1] We also examine whether the growth rate in inflation-adjusted awards per plaintiff appears to have increased at some point during the study period and the growth rates prior to and following any apparent break point.

Throughout this chapter, we discuss trial awards only having non-zero amounts of damages. The expected payment for a verdict depends both on the payment conditional on plaintiff win and the likelihood that the plaintiff will win. Recall from the previous chapter that the plaintiff win rate increased during this period, although how much of the increase was due to social inflation could not be determined. We have also normalized trial awards by the number of plaintiffs to take into account any variation in the number of plaintiffs across cases.

All PI/WD Trial Awards

As shown in the left-hand graph in Figure 5.1, there is no trend in the size of the median inflation-adjusted award per plaintiff between 2010 and 2019 (restricting data to the 15,017 verdicts with positive awards).[2] However, the mean award amount rose considerably—increasing from roughly $2 million per plaintiff in 2019 dollars at the beginning of the period to just under $12 million at the end. The bump in 2014 is driven by two multi-billion-dollar verdicts.[3]

---

[1] The CAGR measures the constant annual growth rate that best reflects the increase in trial awards over the period under consideration. The technique for calculating the CAGR is described in Appendix A.

[2] The award amount includes all types of damages (economic and noneconomic) and is net of any reduction for contributory negligence. The award amounts are for all defendants combined and not apportioned to each defendant.

[3] According to VerdictSearch data, a total of $25.0 billion was awarded to three plaintiffs in 2014 in a Florida state court verdict against tobacco defendants. Punitive damages accounted for $23 billion of the total. In a second 2014 case, $9.5 billion was awarded to two plaintiffs in a case in the U.S. District Court for the Western District of Louisiana. The plaintiff alleged that his bladder cancer was caused by taking

FIGURE 5.1
Award Amount per Plaintiff in PI/WD Tort Cases

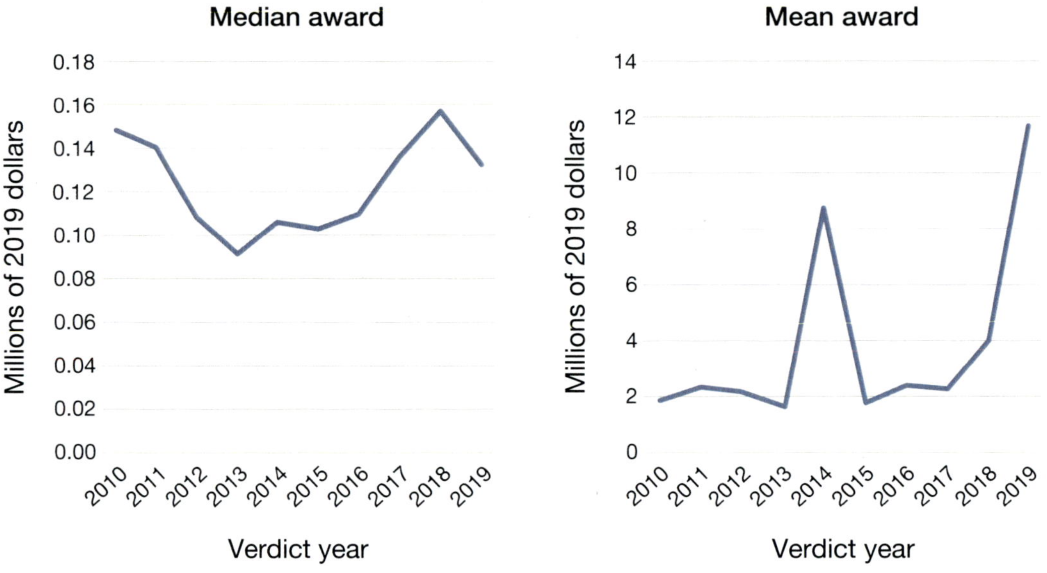

SOURCE: Authors' analysis of 2010–2019 VerdictSearch data.
NOTE: *N* = 15,017 trial awards.

Consistent with trends in the average inflation-adjusted award per plaintiff, the percentage of awards that exceed various dollar thresholds also increased in the latter part of the study period. The percentage of verdicts of $5 million or more per plaintiff in 2019 dollars varied between 5.5 and 7.5 percent between 2010 and 2016 before rising to just under 12 percent in 2019 (see Figure 5.2). The percentage of awards larger than $50 million per plaintiff roughly quadrupled, from 0.4 percent at the beginning of the study period to just under 2 percent by the end.

The percentage of awards that were $5 million or more and the size of the median award suggest that most verdicts are modest in size. As Figure 5.3 shows, more than one-third of the PI/WD trial awards between 2010 and 2019 were less than $50,000 per plaintiff in 2019 dollars, and slightly under one-half were less than $100,000 per plaintiff.

The trends in Figures 5.1 and 5.2 do not consider changes in case characteristics between 2010 and 2019, and we used the statistical approach described in Appendix A to control for these factors.[4] Estimates of the percentage growth in inflation-adjusted trial awards over the previous year are shown in Figure 5.4. These estimates reflect the average percentage change

Actos (pioglitazone hydrochloride), which was made by Takeda Pharmaceuticals Intl, Inc. Punitive damages accounted for $9 billion of the total. Both of these cases fall under the "other cases against organizational defendants" category.

[4] This statistical approach does not use the annual median or mean of trial awards. Instead, it uses all the trial awards in a regression-based approach.

FIGURE 5.2

Trends in the Percentage of Inflation-Adjusted PI/WD Trial Awards That Are Large

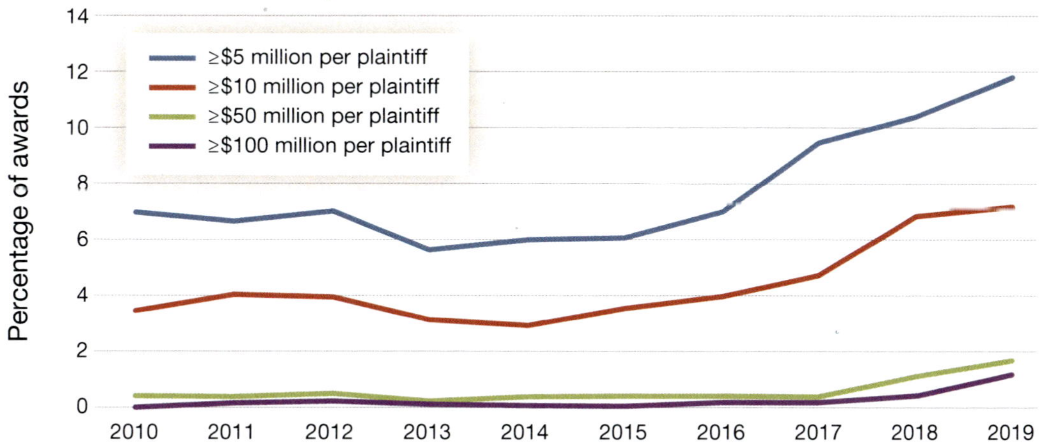

SOURCE: Authors' analysis of 2010–2019 VerdictSearch data.

NOTE: Award and cutoff amounts were adjusted to 2019 dollars using the PCEPI. We define *large* as $5 million or more. *N* = 15,017 trial awards.

FIGURE 5.3

Distribution of Trial Awards per Plaintiff in PI/WD Cases, by Size

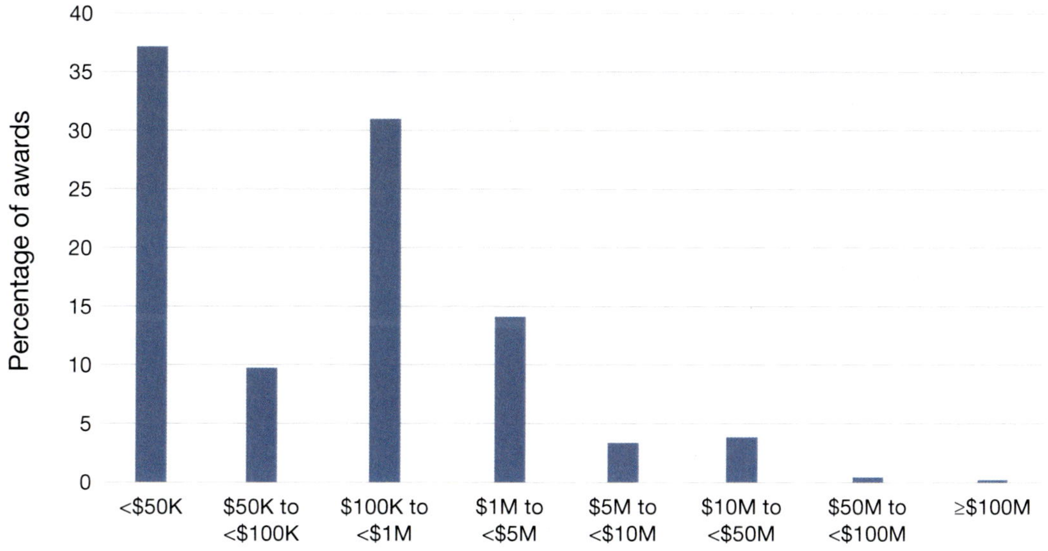

SOURCE: Authors' analysis using 2010–2019 VerdictSearch data.

NOTE: This figure considers all verdicts between 2010 and 2019. Trial awards are shown in 2019 dollars. K = thousand; M = million. *N* = 15,017 trial awards.

FIGURE 5.4

Estimated Percentage Growth in Inflation-Adjusted PI/WD Trial Awards per Plaintiff over the Previous Year, Controlling for Case Characteristics

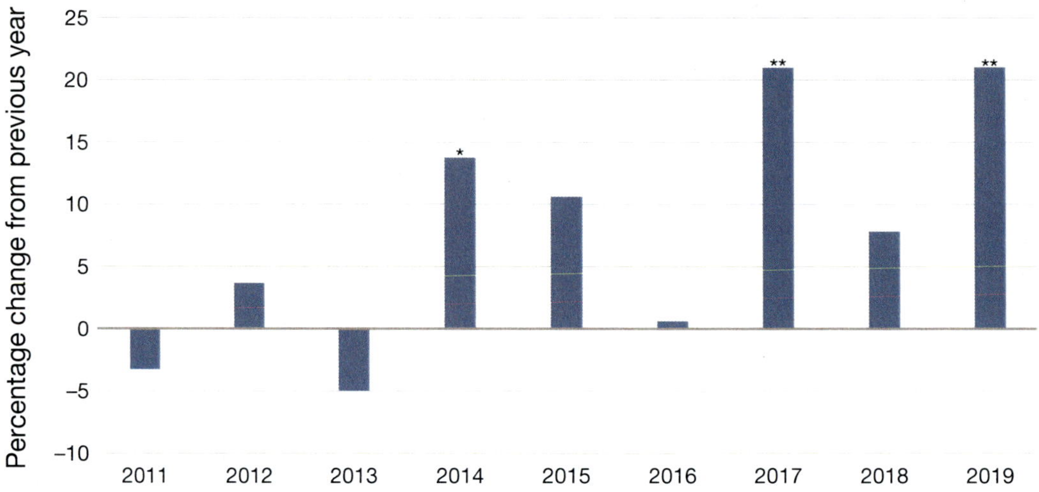

SOURCE: Authors' analysis using 2010–2019 VerdictSearch data.

NOTE: *N* = 15,017 verdicts. * = statistically different from 0 with 90-percent probability; ** = statistically different from 0 with 95-percent probability; *** = statistically different from 0 with 99-percent probability.

across all case types, which, as we discuss in the following section, varies by case type. The figure indicates that trial awards changed little between 2010 and 2013. In 2014, awards began to rise, then they grew at faster rates in subsequent years. The cumulative percentage change in awards (relative to 2010) is shown in Figure 5.5.

Over the entire period, inflation-adjusted awards per plaintiff grew at a 7.6-percent CAGR. The results shown in Figure 5.4 suggest that trial awards began to move upward in 2014, and we estimate the CAGR before and after this dividing point. As shown in Table 5.1, awards tended to fall prior to 2014, but from 2014 on, they rose at an 8.0-percent CAGR.[5]

We explored the sensitivity of the findings to two analytical assumptions. First, we examined the sensitivity of findings to the small number of very large awards. As shown in Table A.2 in Appendix A, the results are not substantially different when the largest awards are trimmed. Second, we examined the sensitivity of findings to the price index used to adjust for inflation. Recall from Chapter 3 that we used the PCEPI to correct for inflation. However, the PCEPI, as a price index, does not account for the change in the quantity of medical care consumed. An increase in the quantity of health care consumed caused by factors outside the tort system would reduce the percentage of the overall increase in trial awards that could be attributed to social inflation. As described in Appendix A, we used trends in per capita

[5] Annual growth from 2014 on is calculated relative to a 2010–2013 baseline period. See Appendix A for details.

FIGURE 5.5

Estimated Growth in Inflation-Adjusted PI/WD Trial Awards per Plaintiff, Controlling for Case Characteristics

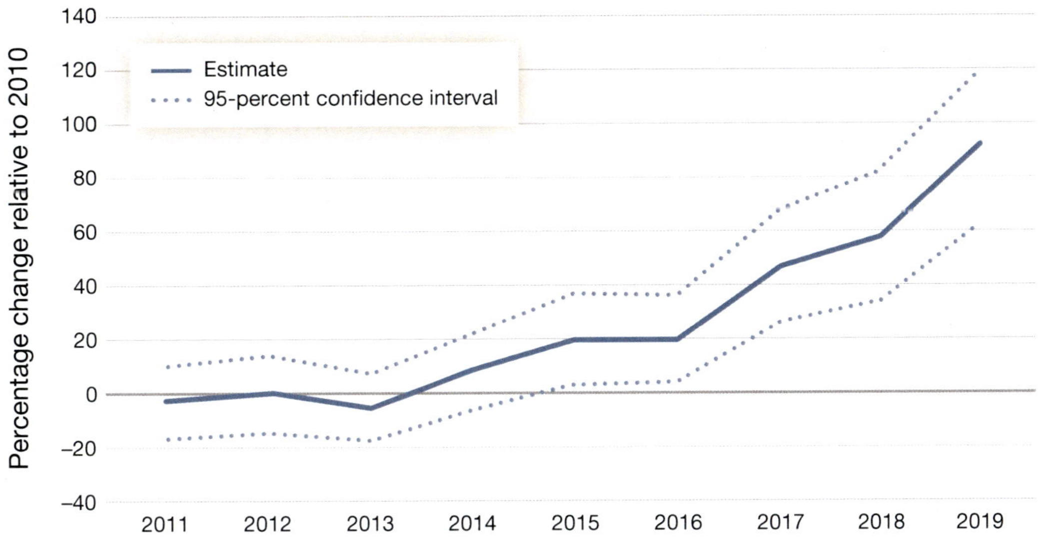

SOURCE: Authors' analysis of 2010–2019 VerdictSearch data.
NOTE: *N* = 15,017 verdicts.

TABLE 5.1

CAGR for PI/WD Inflation-Adjusted Trial Awards per Plaintiff

Verdict Category	*N*	CAGR 2010–2019 (%)	Year Growth Rate Increased	CAGR (%) Pre-Dividing Point	CAGR (%) Post-Dividing Point
All verdicts	15,017	7.6***	2014	–3.8*	8.0***

SOURCE: Authors' analysis of 2010–2019 VerdictSearch data.
NOTE: * = statistically different from 0 with 90-percent probability; ** = statistically different from 0 with 95-percent probability; *** = statistically different from 0 with 99-percent probability.

health care expenditures in the United States as a measure of the change in both price of care and the quantity of care, and we recalculated these findings using an index with a weighted average of the PCEPI and per capita health care expenditures. When each is weighted equally, the CAGR for trial awards between 2010 and 2019 does not change a great deal—falling from 7.6 percent to 6.4 percent (see Table A.3 in Appendix A).[6]

[6] These weights are the same as the weights recommended by Verisk for deflating the severity of BI insurance claims (see Chapter 6).

Trends in Trial Awards by Case Type

The annual growth rate in trial awards might not be uniform across all case types. Thus, in this section, we explore award trends for the following case groupings:

- motor vehicle cases against organizational defendants involving large trucks (referred to as *commercial trucking*)
- motor vehicle cases against organizational defendants not involving large trucks (referred to as *other commercial vehicles*)
- motor vehicle cases against non-organizational defendants (referred to as *private auto*)
- medical malpractice
- other cases against organizational defendants
- other cases against non-organizational defendants.

The number and average and median sizes of trial awards are reported by case type in Appendix B, where we also report change over time in the mix of awards by case type.

Trial awards grew at CAGRs between 8 and 9 percent over the study period for four of the six case types examined (Table 5.2). Growth rates were somewhat slower for awards in medical malpractice and other commercial vehicle cases. The year that award growth rate increases began varied. Growth rates markedly increased for other private auto cases

TABLE 5.2
CAGRs for PI/WD Inflation-Adjusted Trial Awards per Plaintiff, by Case Type

				CAGR (%)	
Case Type	*N*	CAGR 2010–2019 (%)	Year Growth Rate Increased	Pre-Dividing Point	Post-Dividing Point
Organizational defendants	7,971	7.3***	2016	1.2	8.7***
Commercial trucking	683	8.5***	2018	–0.1	19.1***
Other commercial vehicles	2,235	5.1***	2017	2.8	6.2***
Medical malpractice	888	5.7**	2018	1.0	12.4***
Other cases against organizational defendants	4,165	8.8***	2014	–4.3	9.6***
Non-organizational defendants	7,046	8.3***	2014	–2.5	8.6***
Private auto	6,405	8.3***	2014	–0.7	8.4***
Other cases against non-organizational defendants	641	8.1**	2016	–4.2	9.3**

SOURCE: Authors' analysis of 2010–2019 VerdictSearch data.
NOTE: * = statistically different from 0 with 90-percent probability; ** = statistically different from 0 with 95-percent probability; *** = statistically different from 0 with 99-percent probability.

and other cases against organizational defendants in 2014.[7] The large number of awards in these categories drove the increase that began in 2014 for the sample as a whole. Increases occurred later for other case types, in 2016 for other cases against non-organizational defendants and in 2018 for commercial trucking and medical malpractice cases. For both commercial trucking and medical malpractice cases, the growth rate was particularly rapid once the increase in awards began. Awards for commercial trucking were flat between 2010 and 2017, but they grew at nearly a 20-percent annual rate relative to a 2010–2017 baseline period. The experience was similar for medical malpractice awards, which grew at a rate that was not statistically different from zero between 2010 and 2017 but then rose at more than a 12-percent annual rate in 2018 and 2019.

The results do not indicate any substantial difference in the CAGR of cases with organizational and non-organizational defendants. Growth rates exceed 8 percent for both case types involving non-organizational defendants, as well as two of the four case types involving organizational defendants. The year when growth rates increased varied for both groups.

Trends in Trial Awards by Claimed Harm

In this section, we examine trends in trial awards by type of claimed harm. We begin by examining trends by extent of brain injury, then compare trial awards in WD cases with those in PI cases.

Verdicts Involving Brain Injury

Some have asserted that PI cases making their way to trial are increasingly claiming that the plaintiff has serious or long-term consequences from brain trauma or other neurological impairment, even if such conditions appeared to be no more severe than other claimed injuries at the time of the underlying incident. As a result, it is said that such claims would now involve significant future medical costs that were not present in litigation involving similar incidents in years past.[8] Underscoring the potential impact of such assertions, we found that brain injuries were frequently alleged in cases that went to verdict across all six types of cases that we examined (see Table 5.3).

The three left-hand charts in Figure 5.6 report trends over time, controlling for case characteristics, in the percentage of trial awards that involve some sort of brain injury as part of the claim. As shown, the percentage of awards involving what we characterize as "seri-

---

[7] The method used to identify these dividing points is described in Appendix A.

[8] See Craig Beardsley, Erin Collins, Tim Fletcher, Glenn Frankel, Andrew Gifford, and Tom Karol, *Social Inflation Is Complicated and Costly: A Five-Part Series Examining Social Inflation and Its Impact on Insurers*, National Association of Mutual Insurance Companies, NAMIC Issue Analysis, September 2021, p. 12; and Keith M. Rozanski, "Keith Rozanski Moderating Panel Evaluating the Rise of Traumatic Brain Injury Allegations in Hospitality and Retail Personal Injury Claims," Haight, undated.

TABLE 5.3
Frequency of Brain Injury, by Case Type

Case Type	Serious Brain Injury (%)	Other Brain Injury (%)	No Brain Injury (%)
All verdicts	8.3	22.8	68.9
Organizational defendants	11.3	19.6	69.2
Commercial trucking	15.5	20.8	63.8
Other commercial vehicles	9.9	25.6	64.5
Medical malpractice	15.8	19.6	64.6
Other cases against organizational defendants	9.8	17.0	73.2
Non-organizational defendants	4.4	27.0	68.6
Personal auto	4.0	27.8	68.2
Other cases against non-organizational defendants	7.1	21.2	71.7

SOURCE: Authors' analysis of 2010–2019 VerdictSearch data.

ous brain injury" increased modestly over the study period, while the percentage of cases involving other brain injuries increased more substantially. The three right-hand charts in Figure 5.6 show the annual percentage point change in the percentage of trial awards involving brain injuries. There is not an obvious pattern for serious brain injuries, but the percentage point changes for any brain injuries pick up in 2014. The more rapid increase beginning in 2014 coincides with the faster growth rate of trial awards beginning that year and contributes to the increase in inflation-adjusted trial awards between 2010 and 2019.

We found that awards for other brain injuries increased at a 9.5-percent annual growth rate over the study period (see Table 5.4). Trial awards increased more rapidly starting in 2015 for this group of verdicts, but the findings suggest that trial awards were also increasing prior to 2015. In contrast, we found no increase in the inflation-adjusted award per plaintiff in verdicts involving serious brain injuries over the study period. The annual growth rate in trial awards for cases involving serious brain injury between 2010 and 2019 is negative but not statistically different from zero, and there is no evidence that awards increased more rapidly in the latter part of the study period.

FIGURE 5.6

Percentage of Trial Awards Involving Brain Injuries, Controlling for Case Characteristics

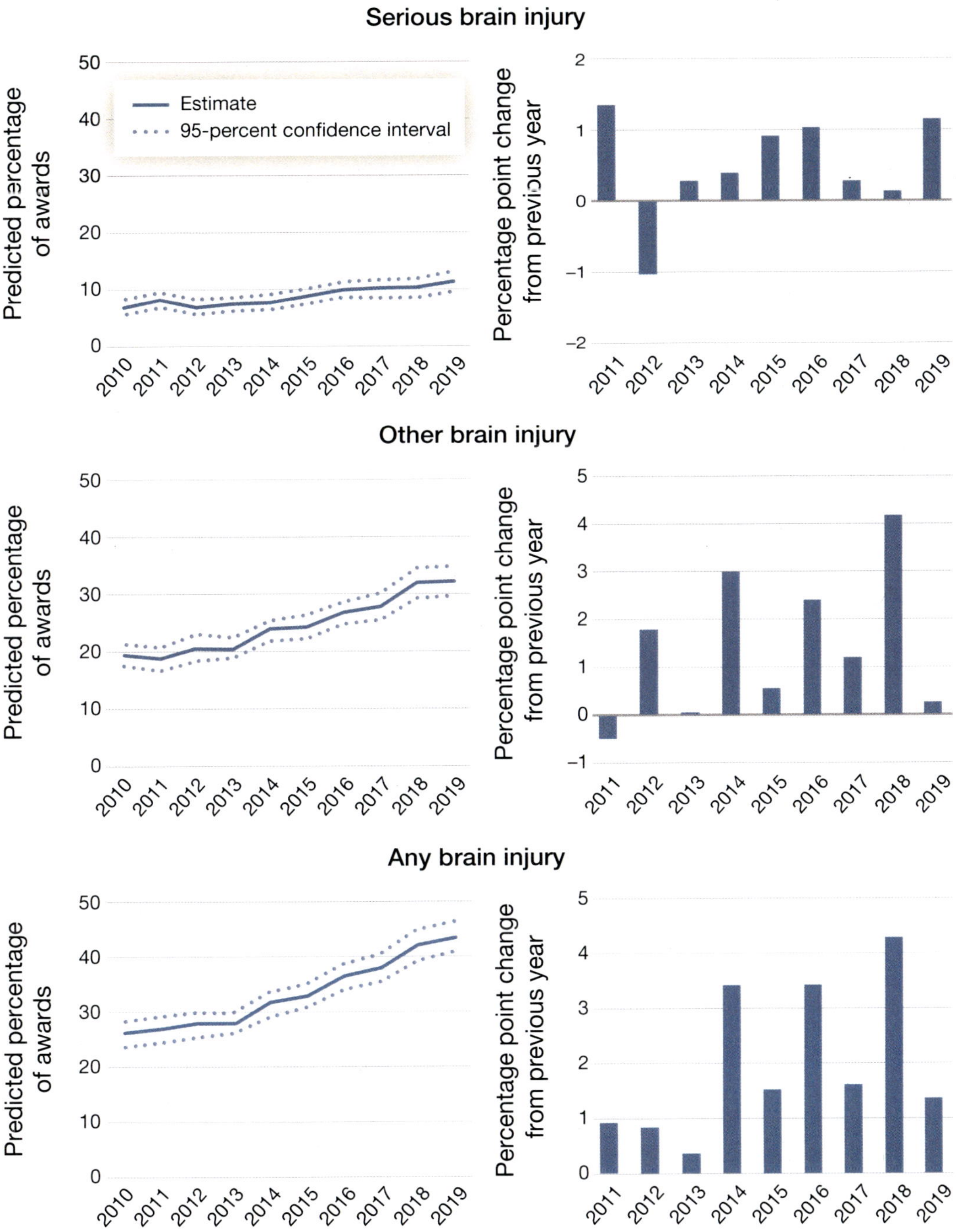

SOURCE: Authors' analysis of 2010–2019 VerdictSearch data.

NOTE: N = 15,017 trial awards.

TABLE 5.4

Annual Growth Rate in PI/WD Inflation-Adjusted Trial Awards per Plaintiff, by Extent of Brain Injury

Extent of Brain Injury	*N*	CAGR 2010–2019 (%)	Year Growth Rate Increased	CAGR (%) Pre-Dividing Point	CAGR (%) Post-Dividing Point
Serious brain injury	1,288	–1.0	None found	—	—
Other brain injury	3,637	9.5***	2015	5.8	9.6***
No brain injury	10,092	6.4***	2014	–4.5**	7.0***

SOURCE: Authors' analysis of 2010–2019 VerdictSearch data.
NOTE: * = statistically different from 0 with 90-percent probability; ** = statistically different from 0 with 95-percent probability; *** = statistically different from 0 with 99-percent probability.

Although the increase in cases involving brain injuries contributed to the growth in inflation-adjusted severity between 2010 and 2019, it does not appear to have been a major cause. When we estimated the increase in the growth rate for all PI/WD awards, controlling for the extent of brain injury in addition to the other factors previously held constant, the estimated CAGR falls from 7.6 percent (see Table 5.1) only to 6.6 percent (see Table A.1 in Appendix A).

Trial Awards in PI Cases Versus WD Cases

Trial awards over the study period appear to have increased somewhat faster in PI cases than in WD cases (see Table 5.5).[9] The growth rate for PI awards also appears to have increased sooner than for WD awards.

TABLE 5.5

Annual Growth in Inflation-Adjusted Trial Awards per Plaintiff, by Case Type

Case Type	*N*	CAGR 2010–2019 (%)	Year Growth Rate Increased	CAGR (%) Pre-Dividing Point	CAGR (%) Post-Dividing Point
PI	13,808	8.1***	2014	–2.2	8.5***
WD	1,209	5.5***	2017	0.3	8.3***

SOURCE: Authors' analysis of 2010–2019 VerdictSearch data.
NOTE: * = statistically different from 0 with 90-percent probability; ** = statistically different from 0 with 95-percent probability; *** = statistically different from 0 with 99-percent probability.

[9] Recall from Chapter 3 that the verdicts we classified as involving wrongful death could also include alleged personal injury to the party that ultimately died or personal injury to a second plaintiff. As shown in Appendix B, trial awards in WD cases tend to be far larger than those in PI cases. However, these tabulations do not control for case type.

Trial Awards by State

Table 5.6 shows the CAGRs for inflation-adjusted trial awards per plaintiff for the seven states with the largest number of plaintiff wins in the VerdictSearch database. Together, these states account for approximately 80 percent of both verdicts and plaintiff wins in our full analysis dataset. Trial awards grew most rapidly in New York, where inflation-adjusted awards per plaintiff grew at 10.4 percent per year over the study period (2010–2019) and growth picked up earlier than in the other six states examined. Growth rates over the study period were of similar magnitude in California, New Jersey, and Texas, although increases in the growth rate came later (2015 in Texas and 2017 in California and New Jersey). It is noteworthy that growth rates were substantial in New York and California even before the pickup in growth seen in 2014 and 2017, respectively. Growth rates over the study period were lower, but still considerable, in Pennsylvania, Illinois, and Florida. The annual growth rate was not large between 2010 and 2019 for the remaining states taken as a whole (2.4 percent), although larger growth rates in some states could be offset by smaller growth rates in others. Like those for the seven states with the largest number of verdicts, the growth rates in the remaining states picked up in the last few years of the study period.

TABLE 5.6

Annual Growth in PI/WD Inflation-Adjusted Trial Awards per Plaintiff, by State

				CAGR (%)	
State	*N*	CAGR 2010–2019 (%)	Year Growth Rate Increased	Pre-Dividing Point	Post-Dividing Point
New York	2,451	10.4***	2014	3.9	11.0***
California	2,013	10.0***	2017	5.3*	12.8***
New Jersey	902	9.2***	2017	1.1	17.9***
Texas	3,171	8.8***	2015	0.9	10.1***
Pennsylvania	1,156	6.1***	2018	3.0	10.2***
Illinois	859	5.8*	2018	3.1	15.0**
Florida	1,465	5.3***	2017	2.3	7.3***
All other states	3,000	2.4	2018	−4.5*	6.4***

SOURCE: Authors' analysis of 2010–2019 VerdictSearch data.
NOTE: "All other states" refers to the remaining 43 U.S. states, the District of Columbia, Puerto Rico, and the U.S. Virgin Islands.
* = statistically different from 0 with 90-percent probability; ** = statistically different from 0 with 95-percent probability;
*** = statistically different from 0 with 99-percent probability.

Discussion

We found that trial awards in PI/WD cases grew faster than the rate of inflation between 2010 and 2019. After adjusting for inflation, trial awards per plaintiff grew at a 7.6-percent CAGR between 2010 and 2019 when verdicts in all states are considered. We also found that the percentage of trial awards exceeding $50 million per plaintiff in 2019 dollars roughly quadrupled over the period, increasing from 0.4 percent to just under 2 percent. We examined the sensitivity of the results under different assumptions meant to capture changes in the quantity of health care provided in addition to price. Under plausible assumptions, we did not find that the results changed a great deal. These findings support the contention that evidence of social inflation is present in our data but is not necessarily conclusive. As discussed in Chapter 4, lower trial rates or declines in the mix and volume of plaintiff verdicts that are reported to VerdictSearch could cause trial awards to increase even absent social inflation.

The results suggest that social inflation is not constant but that it ebbs and flows. For trial awards as a whole, we found that inflation-adjusted awards per plaintiff started to increase in 2014. That finding is consistent with information from other sources. During the course of this project, several insurers and other informed parties with whom we spoke asserted that social inflation accelerated in the mid-2010s. Internet searches also indicate that concern about social inflation picked up at this time. Using the Google Books Ngram Viewer, we found that the use of the term "social inflation" in publications dropped during the Great Recession, then began increasing in 2014.[10] Our Google internet searches for "social inflation," using a custom date range, yielded a modest number of results from 2000 to 2012 by year before jumping in number in 2014. The two very large verdicts in 2014, discussed earlier in this chapter, were perhaps a catalyst for increased attention to social inflation.

The percentage of trial awards in which brain injuries were alleged in the underlying case grew considerably over the study period—rising from 26 percent in 2010 to 44 percent in 2019. This increase could be due to several factors, such as

- a change in the injury mix in cases that ultimately make it to trial
- an improved ability to detect and treat brain injuries
- increased efforts of plaintiff attorneys to highlight possible brain injuries when advancing claims on the part of their clients, perhaps reflecting what they assess to be juries' increased willingness to award compensation for brain injuries of all types.

We found that when a serious brain injury was alleged, awards did not change a great deal over the study period. In contrast, awards in the much larger group of verdicts for cases that alleged less serious brain injuries did grow considerably. The greater room for change

[10] The Google Books Ngram Viewer is a tool that yields the yearly count of user-defined text strings found in Google's scientific literature–focused collection of books and magazines (Google Ngram Viewer Team, "About Ngram Viewer," webpage, undated).

in the assessment of the extent and consequences of less serious brain injuries likely, in part, explains the faster growth for trial awards with these types of injuries. However, we found that the increased frequency of brain injuries contributed only modestly to the growth in trial awards between 2010 and 2019. The role of social inflation in increasing the percentage of cases alleging brain injuries and the amount of compensation awarded when such injuries are alleged deserve further investigation.

Contrary to expectations, we did not find evidence that social inflation affects organizational defendants to a greater degree than non-organizational defendants.[11] However, we did not consider an organization's size in our analysis. It could be that trial awards grew more rapidly for larger organizations than smaller ones. Juror beliefs that individual defendants are backed by large insurance companies could also explain the lack of difference.

We found some support for the notion that the impacts of social inflation vary by case type. The differences in CAGRs across case types are not particularly pronounced, but differences in the timing of the increases in growth rate are more noteworthy. Faster growth appears to have begun sooner for private auto cases and for other cases against organizational defendants. The later increase in awards for commercial trucking is surprising given all the attention paid to this sector, although the growth rate for this case type in the last two years of the study period (2017–2019) is the highest observed.

The results also suggest that social inflation is not occurring equally in all states. The largest increases in inflation-adjusted trial awards and the earliest onsets of more rapid growth were in New York, California, New Jersey, and Texas. Lower increases and later onset dates were observed in Pennsylvania, Illinois, and Florida. There was a much lower increase in the trial awards in the remaining states when grouped together, although larger effects in some states could be offset by smaller effects in others.

---

[11] However, note that similar percentage increases mean much larger dollar increases for organizational defendants given the much higher starting award levels for organizational defendants (see Table A.1 in Appendix A).

CHAPTER 6

Trends in Insurance Claim Severity

Having examined litigation trends and trial awards in Chapters 4 and 5, we now turn to trends in insurance claims. In this chapter, we investigate whether changes in the inflation-adjusted severity of insurance claims are consistent with the expected effects of social inflation. This analysis is based on a very large number on insurance claims and, thus, does not face the same issues as our analysis of trial verdicts, which represent only a very small percentage of the lawsuits filed or insurance claims made. As we will discuss, however, interpretation of the claims data presents its own challenges.

Recall from Chapter 3 that a large majority of the commercial claims in the Verisk database are brought under policies held by small- and medium-sized businesses. The limits on these policies are predominantly $1 million/$2 million. The policy limits on the personal auto policies for which we have data vary by state but usually do not exceed $100,000/$300,000. (We refer to both of these, going forward, as *baseline policy limits.*)

In the first part of this chapter, we examine trends in the inflation-adjusted severity of claims brought under policies that typically have these limits. Verisk has more-limited data on policies with higher limits, which are typically held by larger firms. In the second part of this chapter, we investigate the extent to which claim costs for these higher-limit policies grew faster than for lower-limit policies.

Inflation-Adjusted Claim Severity for Baseline Policy Limits

We begin by examining trends in the inflation-adjusted severity of BI claims, then turn to PD claims. The losses underlying BI claims align more closely with those that characterize the trial awards examined in preceding chapters than do PD claims. In contrast to the analysis in the previous chapter, which was based on trial awards per plaintiff, the analysis in this chapter is based on average claim severity by accident year.

BI Claims

The severity of the BI claims has increased considerably since 2001. As the four left-hand charts in Figure 6.1 show, inflation-adjusted severity was between 40 and 50 percent higher in 2019 than in 2001 for CGL, premises and operations claims; CGL, products and completed operations claims; and third-party commercial auto claims. Data on third-party personal

FIGURE 6.1
Severity of BI Claims, 2001–2020

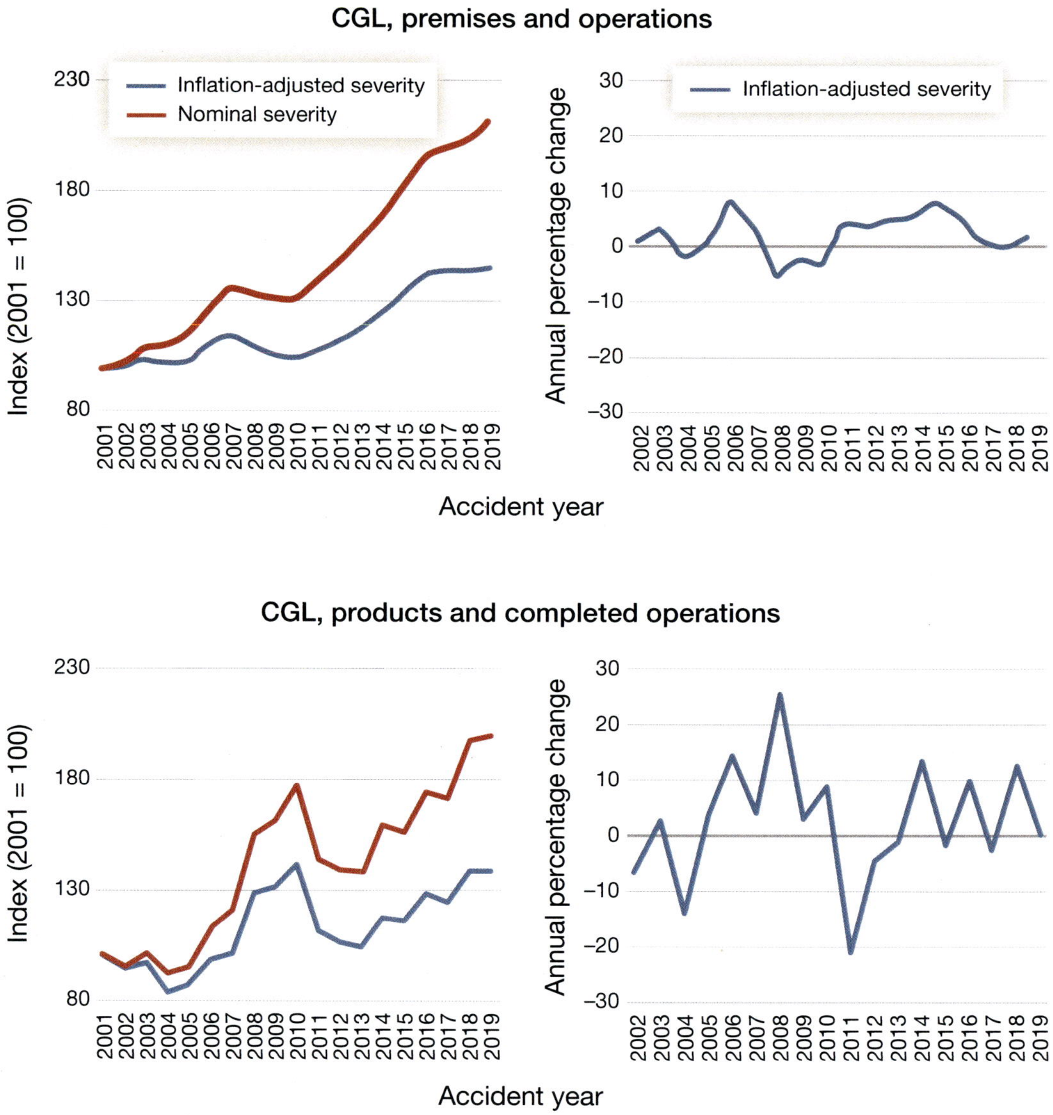

Figure 6.1—Continued

Third-party commercial auto

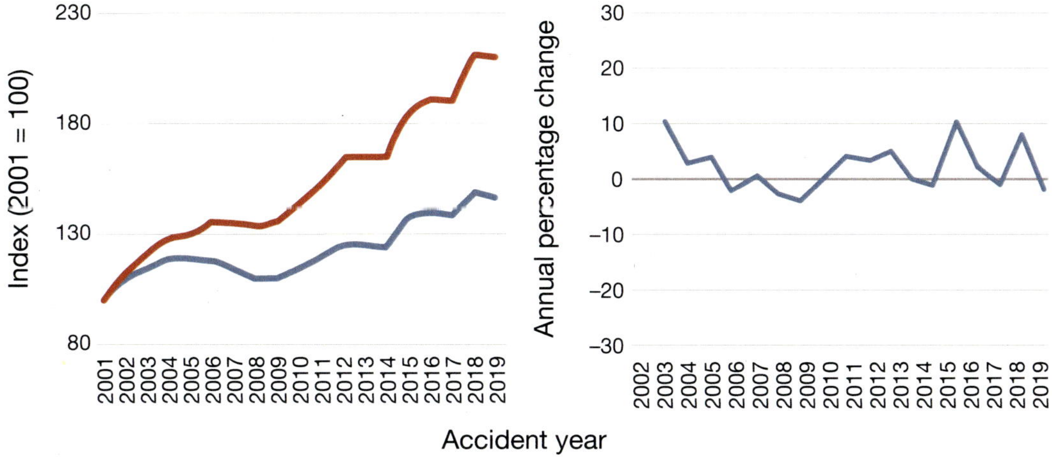

Third-party personal auto

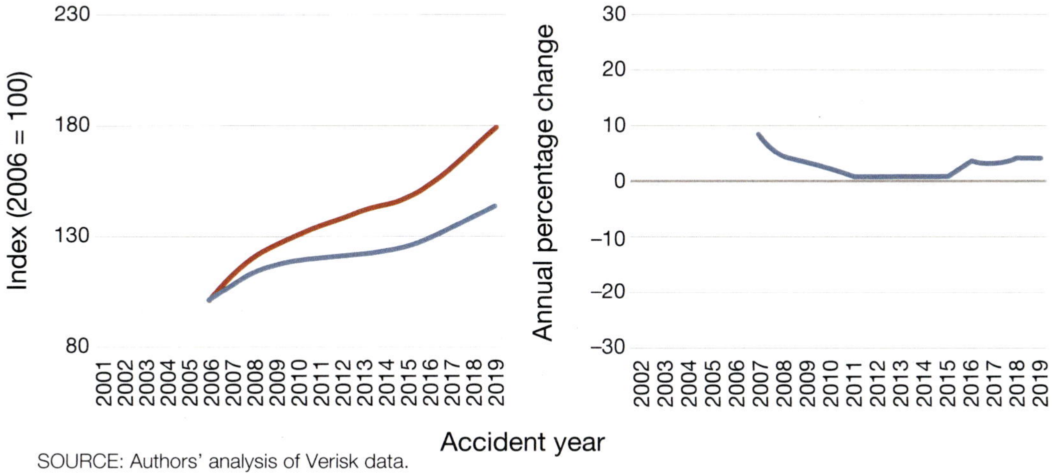

SOURCE: Authors' analysis of Verisk data.

auto claims were available only beginning in 2006 and show that claims grew about 40 percent between 2006 and 2019. The four right-hand charts in Figure 6.1 show the year-over-year percentage change in the indices.

Growth Rates in Claim Severity for All BI Market Segments Combined

Table 6.1 shows the CAGR in inflation-adjusted severity for BI claims between 2001 and 2019 when all four BI market segments are considered together. The statistical approach for doing so is similar to that used for the analysis presented in Chapter 5, which we describe in Appendix A. Because available data for personal auto claims begin in 2006, the second column of the table reports the CAGR for such claims only between 2010 and 2019. The third column excludes personal auto claims from the analysis and reports the CAGRs both for 2001–2010 and the study period (2010–2019).

As Table 6.1 shows, the severity of BI claims grew faster than inflation both between 2001 and 2019 and between 2010 and 2019. The growth rate was somewhat higher in the 2010s than in the 2000s, but at roughly 3 percent, the CAGR between 2010 and 2019 is lower than the 7.6-percent CAGR observed over the same period for PI/WD trial awards (see Table 5.1 in Chapter 5).

Recall from Chapter 5 that we found little change in trial awards between 2010 and 2013, then found considerable growth from 2014 through 2019. The next two figures explore whether the pattern is similar for the inflation-adjusted severity of BI claims. Figure 6.2 shows the estimated growth in inflation-adjusted severity for BI claims between 2010 and 2019 when all four BI market segments are considered together, and Figure 6.3 shows the year-over-year percentage changes. Similar to the findings for trial awards, there appears to be little change in severity between 2010 and 2013 and growth in severity from 2014 on. Note,

TABLE 6.1

CAGRs for the Inflation-Adjusted Severity of BI Claims

	CAGR (%)	
Period	Includes Personal Auto[a]	Excludes Personal Auto[b]
2001–2010	—	2.0***
2010–2019	2.7***	3.0***
2001–2019	—	2.0***

SOURCE: Authors' analysis of Verisk data.
NOTE: * = statistically different from 0 with 90-percent probability; ** = statistically different from 0 with 95-percent probability; *** = statistically different from 0 with 99-percent probability.

[a] Based on annual observations of severity between 2010 and 2019 for the following four market segments: CGL, premises and operations; CGL, products and completed operations; third-party commercial auto; and third-party personal auto.

[b] Based on annual observations of severity between 2001 and 2019 for the following three market segments: CGL, premises and operations; CGL, products and completed operations; and third-party commercial auto.

FIGURE 6.2

Estimated Growth in the Inflation-Adjusted Severity of BI Claims

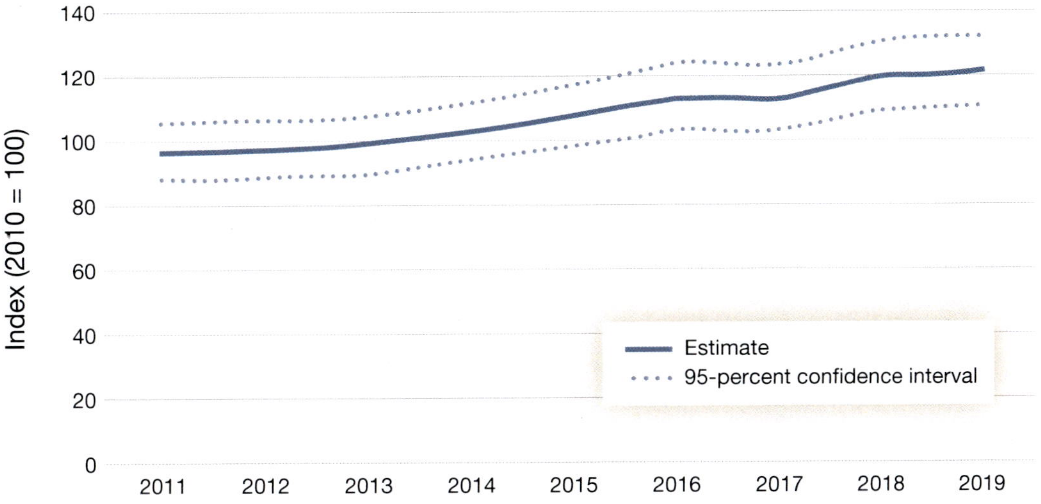

SOURCE: Authors' analysis of Verisk data.

NOTE: The estimate is based on annual observations of severity between 2010 and 2019 for the following four market segments: CGL, premises and operations; CGL, products and completed operations; third-party commercial auto; and third-party personal auto.

FIGURE 6.3

Percentage of Change from the Previous Year in the Inflation-Adjusted Severity of BI Claims

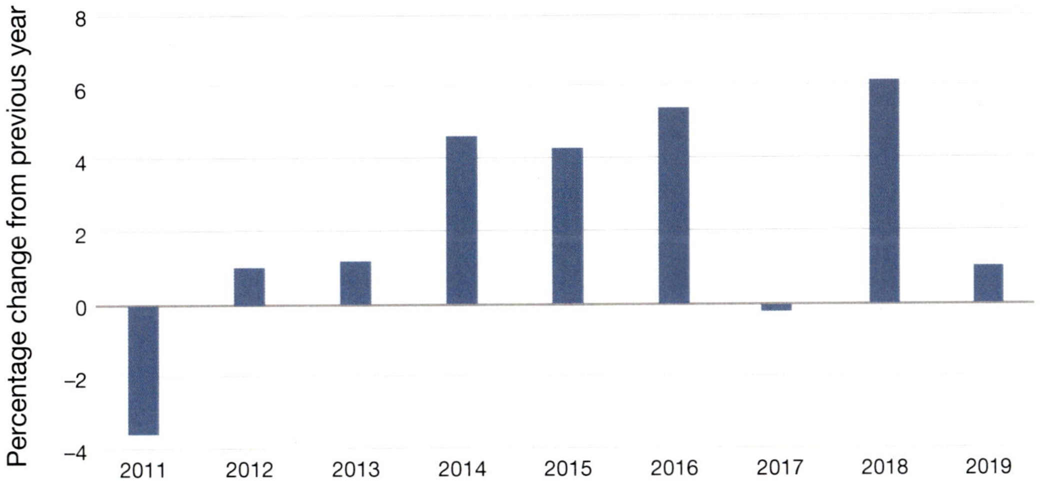

SOURCE: Authors' analysis of Verisk data.

NOTE: None of the changes are statistically different from 0 with 90-percent probability. These results are based on annual observations of severity between 2010 and 2019 for the following four market segments: CGL, premises and operations; CGL, products and completed operations; third-party commercial auto; and third-party personal auto.

however, that this analysis is based on a small number of annual observations and that none of the differences reported in Figure 6.3 is statistically different from zero.

Although the pattern of growth in the inflation-adjusted severity of BI claims lines up with that for trial awards, the pace of growth from 2014 on is lower. As shown in Table 6.2, the inflation-adjusted severity for BI claims grew at approximately 3.5 percent between 2014 and 2019, which was less than one-half of the 8.0-percent CAGR for trial awards (see Table 5.1 in Chapter 5).

Recall from Chapter 2 that the BI price index used to convert claim severity into 2019 dollars is an average of the overall PCEPI and the PCEPI medical care component. This index does not consider changes in the quantity of medical care consumed. Similar to our approach for trial verdicts, we recalculated the results, replacing the PCEPI medical care component with an index for U.S. medical expenditures per capita. When recalculated in this way, the CAGR (including personal auto claims) falls from 3.5 percent between 2014 and 2019 to 2.3 percent (see Table A.4 in Appendix A).

Growth Rates in BI Claim Severity by Market Segment

Claim severity grew faster than inflation in all four BI market segments considered. Inflation-adjusted severity for the two CGL market segments and third-party commercial auto all grew at roughly a 2-percent CAGR between 2001 and 2019 (see the bottom row of Table 6.3). The inflation-adjusted severity of third-party personal auto BI claims also grew 2 percent per year between 2010 and 2019. The tables show that the CAGR between 2010 and 2019 for the organizational policyholders of third-party commercial auto claims is only slightly higher than that for the non-organizational policyholders of third-party personal auto claims (3 percent versus 2 percent, respectively). This finding reinforces our inference (discussed in Chapter 5) that firm size, not status as an organizational defendant alone, might be most relevant to the effects of social inflation.

TABLE 6.2

CAGRs for the Inflation-Adjusted Severity of BI Claims, Before and After 2014

	CAGR (%)	
Period	Includes Personal Auto[a]	Excludes Personal Auto[b]
2010–2013	−0.4	−0.8
2014–2019	3.5***	3.8***

SOURCE: Authors' analysis of Verisk data.

NOTE: * = statistically different from 0 with 90-percent probability; ** = statistically different from 0 with 95-percent probability; *** = statistically different from 0 with 99-percent probability.

[a] Based on annual observations of severity between 2010 and 2019 for the following four market segments: CGL, premises and operations; CGL, products and completed operations; third-party commercial auto; and third-party personal auto.

[b] Based on annual observations of severity between 2010 and 2019 for the following three market segments: CGL, premises and operations; CGL, products and completed operations; and third-party commercial auto.

TABLE 6.3
CAGRs for the Inflation-Adjusted Severity of BI Claims, by Market Segment

	CAGR (%)			
Period	CGL, Premises and Operations	CGL, Products and Completed Operations	Third-Party Commercial Auto	Third-Party Personal Auto
2001–2010	0.9**	4.7***	0.5	—
2010–2019	4.3***	1.7	3.0***	2.0***
2001–2019	2.2***	2.1***	1.7***	—

SOURCE: Authors' analysis of Verisk data.
NOTE: * = statistically different from 0 with 90-percent probability; ** = statistically different from 0 with 95-percent probability; *** = statistically different from 0 with 99-percent probability.

Trial awards rose particularly rapidly in PI/WD cases involving trucks, tractors, and trailers against organizational defendants, and we now turn to trends in claim severities for this market segment. Verisk provided separate data for third-party commercial auto—trucks, tractors, and trailers, and for third-party commercial auto—private passenger vehicle types. These market segments include both BI and PD claims, although BI claims account for roughly 75 percent of the total payments. As the two left-hand charts in Figure 6.4 show, the inflation-adjusted severity for both market segments increased by roughly 80 percent between 2001 and 2019. The two right-hand charts in Figure 6.4 show the year-over-year percentage change in the indices.

Inflation-adjusted severity grew at modest CAGRs for both vehicle types between 2001 and 2010 (1.1 percent for trucks, tractors, and trailers and 0.2 percent for private passenger vehicle types), then increased to 4.8 and 5.4 percent, respectively, between 2010 and 2019 (see Table 6.4). These growth rates are somewhat higher than the growth rates between 2001 and 2019 for the other market segments so far considered. However, the 4.8-percent CAGR for trucks, tractors, and trailers between 2010 and 2019 is less than the 8.5-percent CAGR for commercial trucking trial awards over the same period (see Table 5.2 in Chapter 5). The 5.4-percent CAGR for commercial auto claims involving private passenger vehicle types between 2010 and 2019 is comparable to the 5.1-percent CAGR for trial awards involving other commercial vehicles.

PD Claims

PD claims are more straightforward to quantify than BI claims and, thus, presumably less affected by changes in juror attitudes or tort system rules and practices.[1] The trial awards that we examined were only for PI/WD cases, so we were unable to compare trends in trial awards

[1] An exception to this rule might be business-interruption policies. See Dixon and Morikawa, 2021, for a discussion of business-interruption policies in the context of structuring an insurance program for pandemic risk.

FIGURE 6.4

Severity of Third-Party Commercial Auto Claims, by Vehicle Type

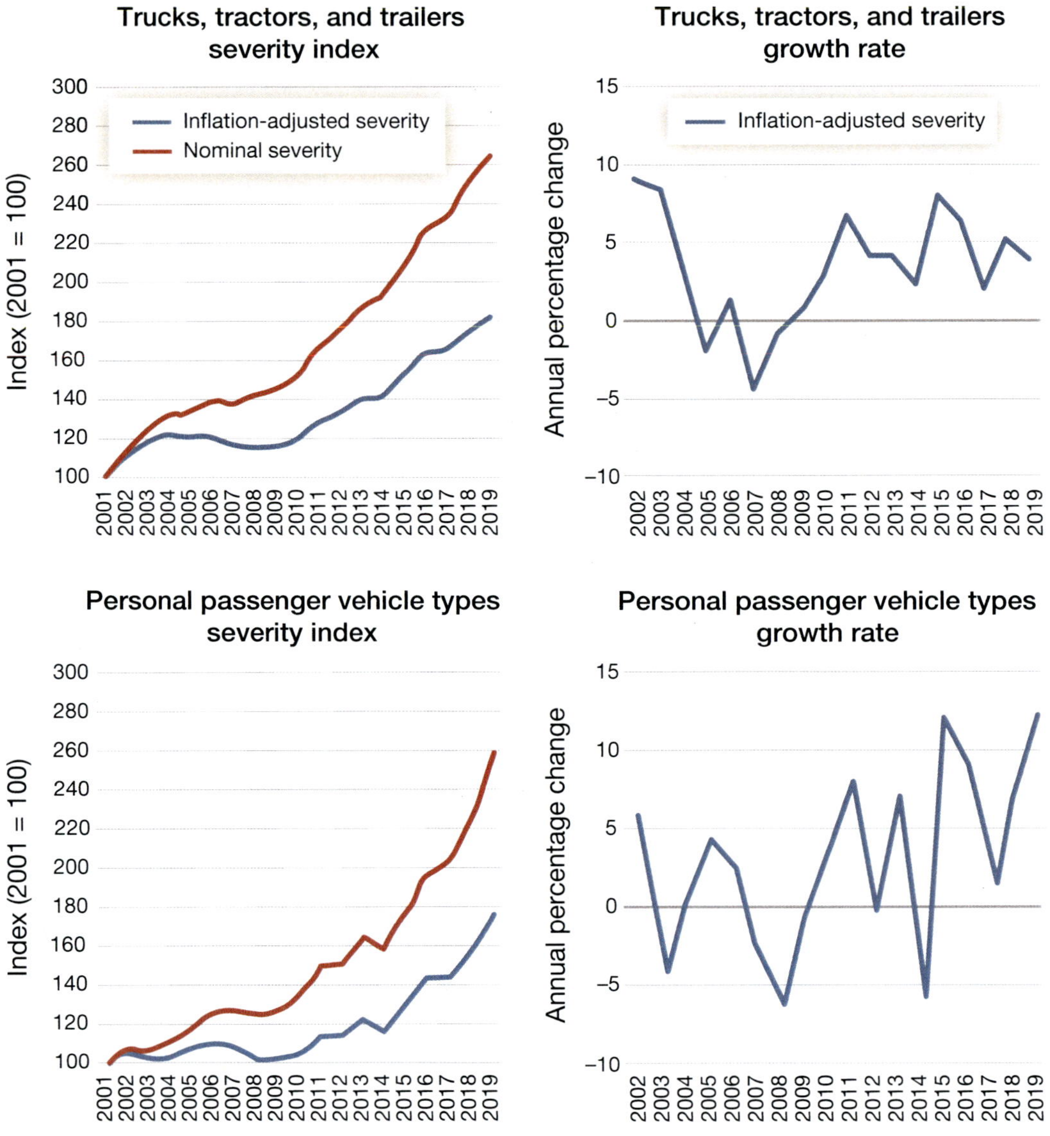

SOURCE: Authors' analysis of Verisk data.

TABLE 6.4

CAGRs for the Inflation-Adjusted Severity of Commercial Auto Claims, by Vehicle Type

	CAGR (%)	
Period	Trucks, Tractors, and Trailers	Private Passenger Vehicle Types
2001–2010	1.1*	0.2
2010–2019	4.8***	5.4***
2001–2019	2.8***	2.6***

SOURCE: Authors' analysis of Verisk data.
NOTE: * = statistically different from 0 with 90-percent probability; ** = statistically different from 0 with 95-percent probability; *** = statistically different from 0 with 99-percent probability.

for PI/WD cases with cases that do not allege personal injury or wrongful death. However, Verisk was able to provide separate data on PD claims, and in this section, we compare the growth rates in severity for PD claims across seven market segments with the growth rates for BI claims. Trends in the severity of PD claims are shown in the seven left-hand charts in Figure 6.5 for the following market segments:

- CGL, premises and operations
- CGL, products and completed operations
- third-party commercial auto
- first-party commercial auto
- commercial property (excluding catastrophic events)
- third-party personal auto
- first-party personal auto.

The seven right-hand charts in Figure 6.5 show the year-over-year percentage change in the indices.

FIGURE 6.5
Severity of PD Claims, 2010–2019

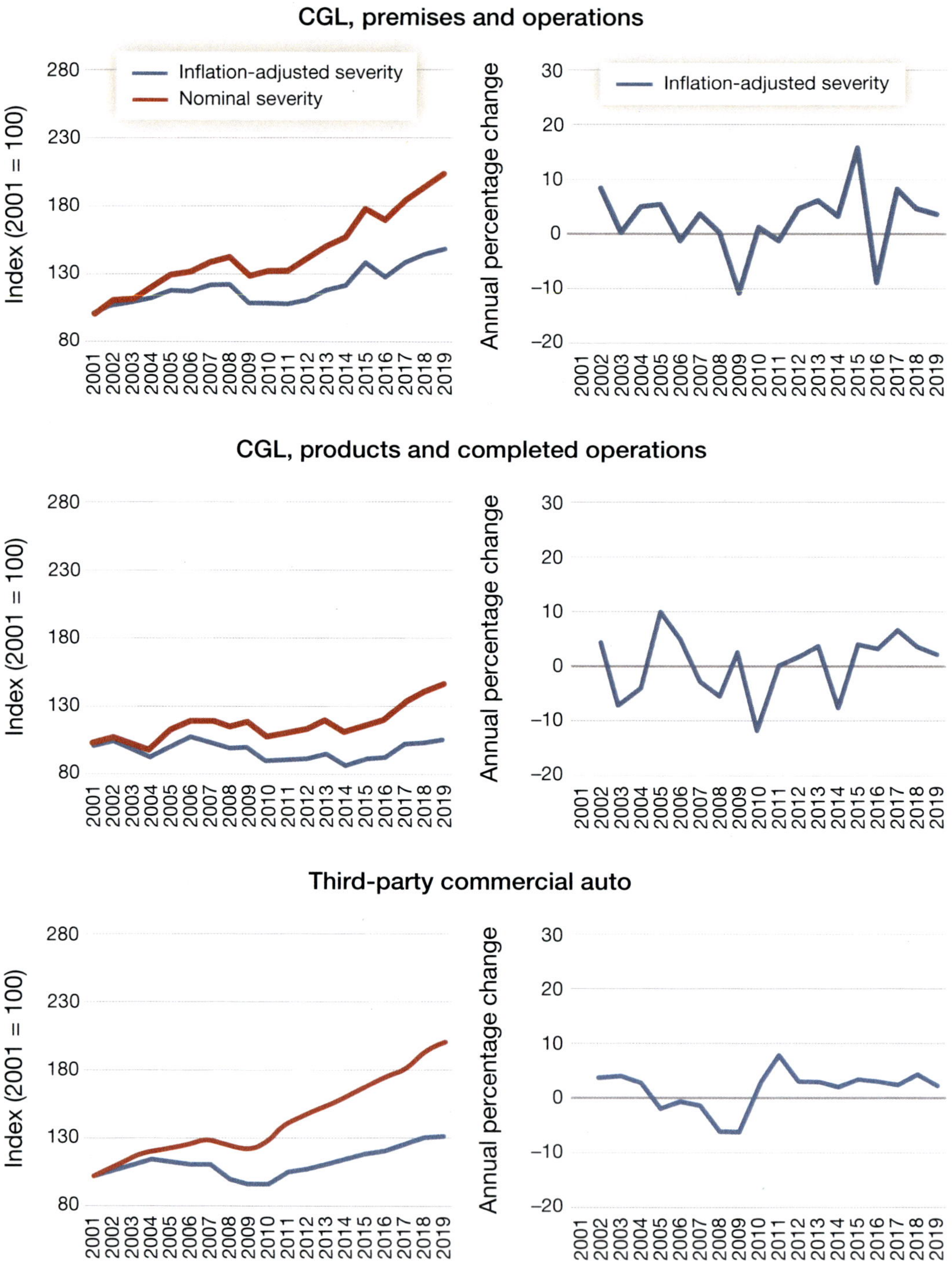

Figure 6.5—Continued

First-party commercial auto

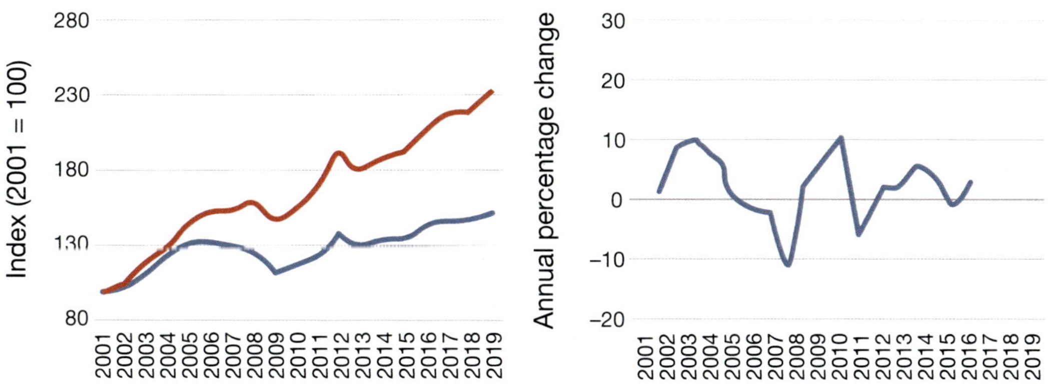

Commercial property (excluding catastrophic events)

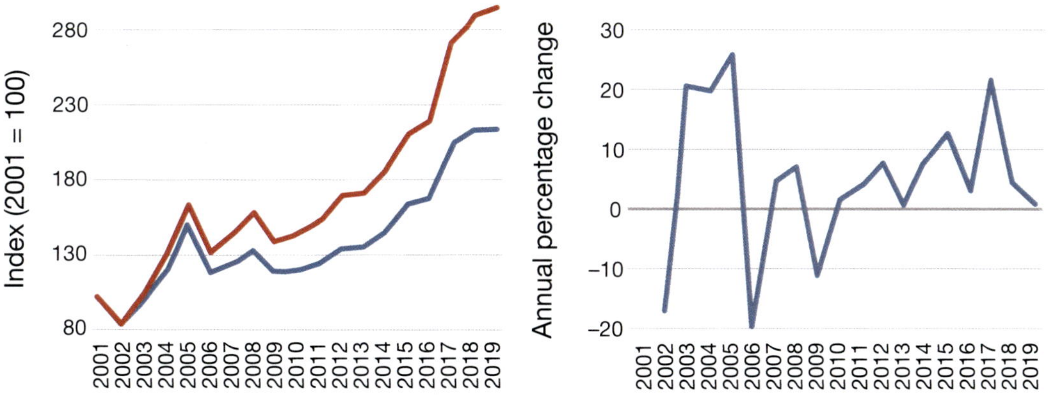

Third-party personal auto

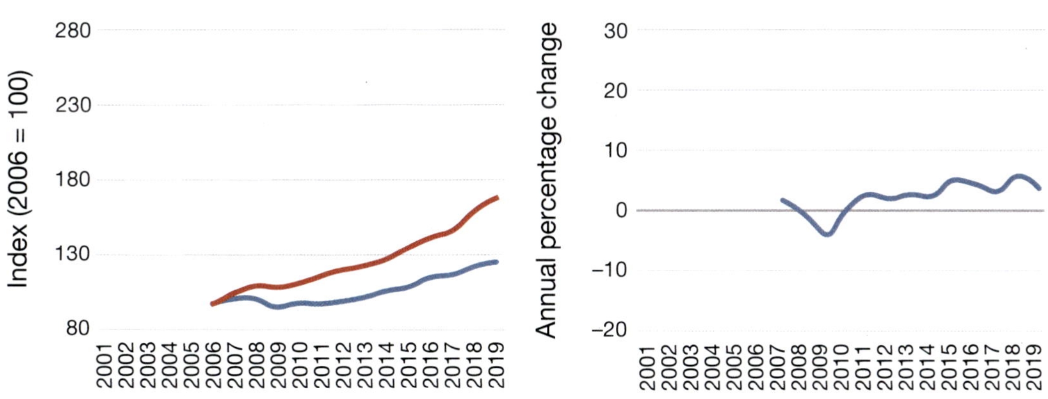

Figure 6.5—Continued

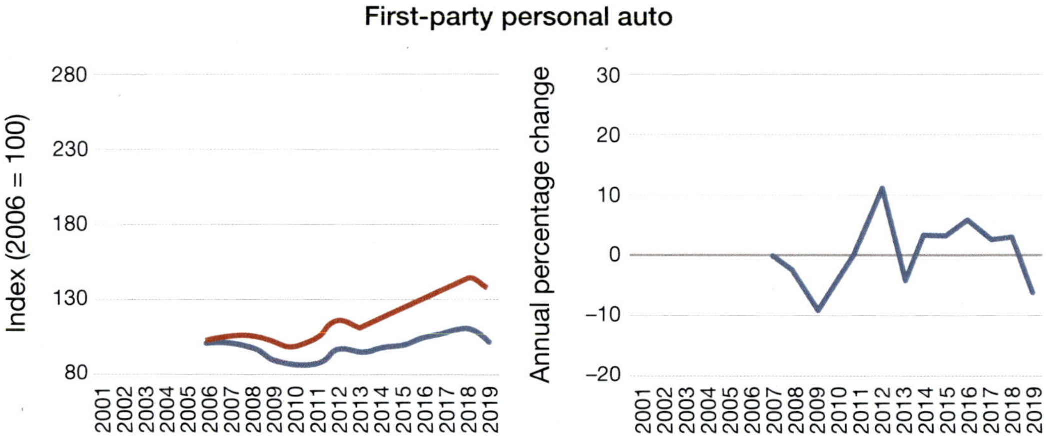

SOURCE: Authors' analysis of Verisk data.

The CAGRs between 2001 and 2010, between 2010 and 2019, and between 2001 and 2019 are shown for each market segment in Table 6.5.

Combining the data for all seven market segments, we find that inflation-adjusted severity grew faster in the 2010s than in the 2000s (see Table 6.6). At 3.5 percent, the CAGR for PD claims between 2010 and 2019 differs little from the 2.7-percent CAGR for BI claims (see Table 6.1) over the same period.

In contrast to the findings for BI claims, growth in the inflation-adjusted severity of PD claims does not appear to be correlated with the growth in trial verdicts. Figures 6.6 and 6.7 show the estimated growth in inflation-adjusted severity when all seven PD market segments

TABLE 6.5
CAGRs for the Inflation-Adjusted Severity of PD Claims, by Market Segment

	Third-Party Claim CAGR (%)				First-Party Claim CAGR (%)		
Period	CGL, P&O	CGL, P&CO	Commercial Auto	Personal Auto	Commercial Auto	Personal Auto	Commercial Property[a]
2001–2010	0.9	−0.5	−1.0	—	1.8*	—	3.4**
2010–2019	3.8***	1.8***	3.3***	3.1***	2.6***	2.7***	7.5***
2001–2019	1.6***	−0.2	1.1***	—	1.8***	—	4.2***

SOURCE: Authors' analysis of Verisk data.
NOTE: * = statistically different from 0 with 90-percent probability; ** = statistically different from 0 with 95-percent probability; *** = statistically different from 0 with 99-percent probability. P&CO = products and completed operations; P&O = premises and operations.
[a] Excludes catastrophic events.

TABLE 6.6

Combined CAGRs for the Inflation-Adjusted Severity of PD Claims

	CAGR (%)	
Period	**Includes Personal Auto[a]**	**Excludes Personal Auto[b]**
2001–2010	—	0.9**
2010–2019	3.5***	3.8***
2001–2019	—	1.7***

SOURCE: Authors' analysis of Verisk data.
NOTE: * = statistically different from 0 with 90-percent probability; ** = statistically different from 0 with 95-percent probability; *** = statistically different from 0 with 99-percent probability.

[a] Based on annual observations of severity between 2010 and 2019 for the following seven market segments: CGL, premises and operations; CGL, products and completed operations; third-party commercial auto; first-party commercial auto; commercial property (excluding catastrophic events); third-party personal auto; and first-party personal auto.

[b] Based on annual observations of severity between 2001 and 2019 for the following five market segments: CGL, premises and operations; CGL, products and completed operations; third-party commercial auto; first-party commercial auto; and commercial property (excluding catastrophic events).

FIGURE 6.6

Estimated Growth in the Inflation-Adjusted Severity of PD Claims

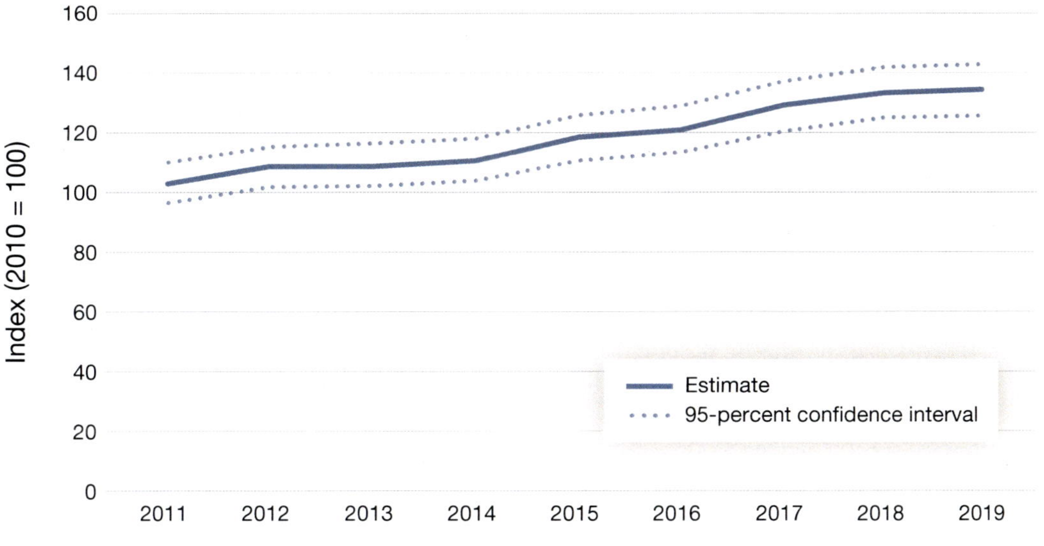

SOURCE: Authors' analysis of Verisk data.
NOTE: N = 70 annual observations of average inflation-adjusted severity.

FIGURE 6.7

Percentage Growth from the Previous Year in the Inflation-Adjusted Severity of PD Claims

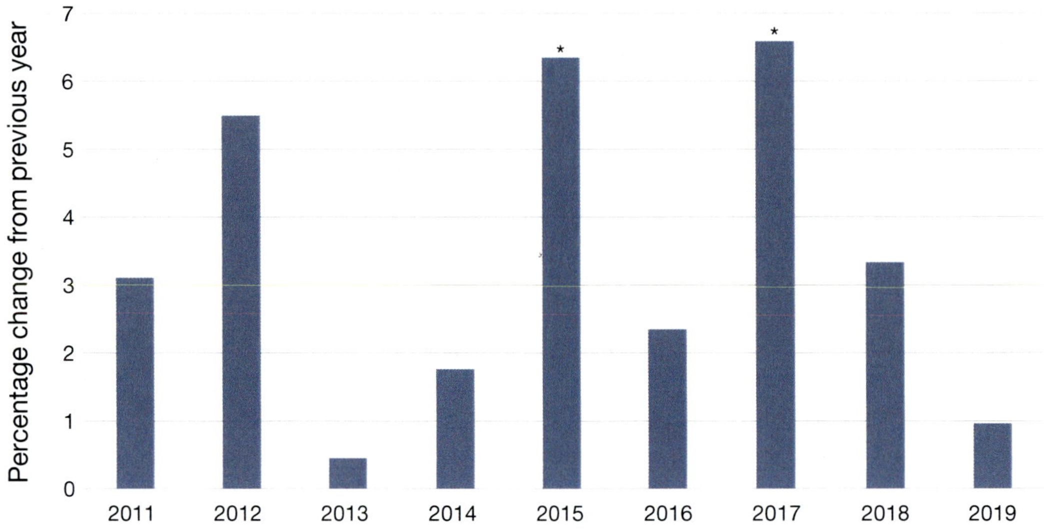

SOURCE: Authors' analysis of Verisk data.

NOTE: N = 70 annual observations of inflation-adjusted severity. * = statistically different from 0 with 90-percent probability; ** = statistically different from 0 with 95-percent probability; *** = statistically different from 0 with 99-percent probability.

are considered together, along with the estimated annual percentage change. As Figure 6.7 shows, the growth rate of PD claim severity does not appear to pick up in 2014 as it did for trial awards and BI claims (see Figure 5.4 in Chapter 5 for trial awards and Figure 6.3 for BI claims).

Claim Severity of Higher-Limit Policies

The results so far in this chapter reflect trends in claim severity *for policies that predominantly do not exceed baseline policy limits* ($1 million/$2 million for commercial policies and $100,000/$300,000 for personal auto policies). In this section, we examine trends in severity of policies with higher limits than these (i.e., *higher-limit policies*). Such policies are typically held by larger firms. If social inflation affects larger firms to a greater degree than smaller firms, we would expect claim severity to grow faster for higher-limit policies than for those examined thus far. If social inflation affects firms of all sizes equally, the data could still show severity to be growing faster for higher-limit policies if claim amounts for the lower-limit policies were increasingly bumping up against policy limits, thus limiting the observed growth in severity. In this case, the growth rate for higher-limit policies would equal the growth in the insured-plus-uninsured losses for policyholders with lower-limit policies.[2]

[2] This argument ignores deductible costs.

The claims experience for higher-limit policies are included in the data that Verisk compiles, and in this section, we use these data to investigate the growth in inflation-adjusted severities for such policies. We first describe the analytic approach, then turn to the findings.

Analytic Approach

Verisk uses claims data on policies with varying limits to produce increased limit factors (ILFs). ILFs allow an insurer to estimate how much greater loss would cost, for example, if the policy limit increased from $1 million to $2 million per occurrence. Claim frequency is assumed not to be affected by policy limit, so these ILFs do not reflect any change in frequency as the policy limit increases, only a change in severity.[3]

To determine the extent to which claim severity is increasing more rapidly for higher-limit policies, we first calculated the ratio of the claim severity of policies with a given occurrence limit to that of policies with a lower occurrence limit. For example, the ILF ratio when increasing a policy limit from $1 million per occurrence to $2 million per occurrence would be the ratio of the claim severity of a policy with a $2 million limit to the claim severity of a policy with a $1 million limit. We then calculated the CAGR in these ratios over time. If severity grew proportionally for all policy limits, the growth rates would be zero. Positive growth rates indicate that severity is growing faster for policies with higher limits. Available Verisk data allowed us to calculate growth in the ILF ratios between 2012 and 2019, and Figure 6.8 shows ILF ratios for commercial liability policies (both BI and PD claims) in 2012 and 2019. BI claims account for approximately 75 percent of commercial auto claims. ILFs are calculated separately for different vehicle classes—in this case, light and medium, heavy, and extra heavy vehicles. Figure 6.8 shows ILF ratios for heavy commercial vehicles. The data that we used to analyze ILFs were not broken down by state, and we adjusted both claim severity and the policy limits for inflation. For heavy vehicles, claim severity in 2019 increased by approximately 15 percent when the limit increased from $1 million to $2 million per occurrence. Severity is roughly 60 percent higher when the limit per occurrence increases from $1 million to $20 million. Verisk claims that it has sufficient data to calculate ILFs up to occurrence limits of $50 million.[4] As Figure 6.8 shows, the ILF ratios increased between 2012 and 2019.

ILFs are based on claims occurring over the previous 14 years (8 years for the auto market segments) that closed in the most recent 5 years. ILFs for 2019 will therefore be based on claims that closed between 2015 and 2019, and ILFs for 2016 will be based on claims that

[3] The ILFs that we considered in this analysis are distinct from the ILFs that Verisk files with state rating agencies. In particular, the ILFs considered do not include risk loads that are typically added to such filings to compensate insurers for the risk associated with higher-limit policies. Rather, the ILFs are based on the severity of claims brought under the policies.

[4] Verisk representative, discussion with the authors, 2023.

FIGURE 6.8
Increased Limit Factor Ratios for Heavy Commercial Vehicles in 2012 and 2019

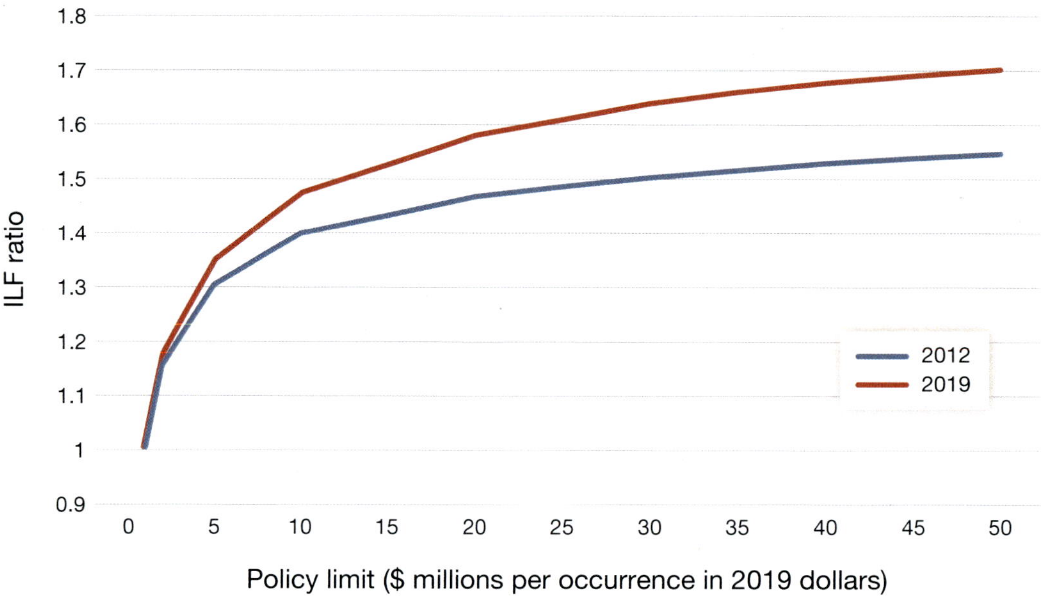

SOURCE: Authors' analysis of Verisk data.

closed between 2012 and 2016. As discussed earlier in this chapter, we found some evidence that claim severity for BI claims began growing at a faster rate in 2014. Because 2014 falls in the middle of the year range used to calculate ILFs for 2016, we chose to compare CAGRs for ILF ratios between 2012 and 2015 with CAGRs between 2015 and 2019.

Findings

CAGRs for ILF ratios for commercial auto liability (BI and PD claims combined) between 2012 and 2015 and between 2015 and 2019 are shown in Figure 6.8. As shown, ILF ratios declined or grew only slightly between 2012 and 2015. In contrast, ILF ratios grew more rapidly between 2015 and 2019. For example, the CAGRs for higher-limit policies were between 2 and 3 percent for light and medium and heavy vehicles and between 3 and 4 percent for extra heavy vehicles (Figure 6.9).

The severity of a higher-limit policy is the product of the severity of the baseline limit layer (i.e., $1 million per occurrence) and the ILF ratio, and the growth in severity of the higher-limit policy is approximately the sum of the growth rates for the baseline limit layer and the ILF ratio

FIGURE 6.9
CAGRs for ILF Ratios for Commercial Auto Claims, by Vehicle Type

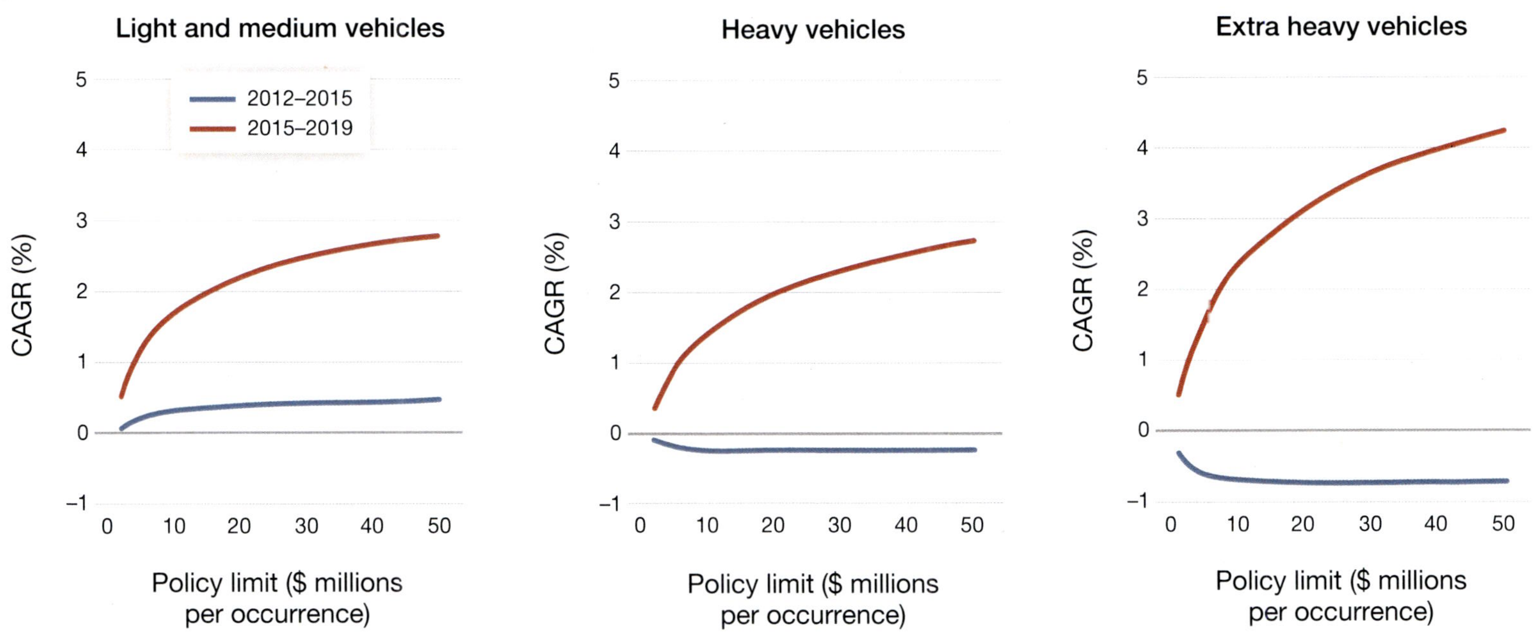

SOURCE: Authors' analysis of Verisk data.

when the growth rates for the baseline limit layer and the ILF ratios are moderate.[5] Previously in this chapter, we found that the CAGR for commercial auto—trucks, tractors, and trailers claim severity (when policy limits are predominantly $1 million per occurrence) was approximately 5 percent between 2010 and 2019 (see Table 6.4). The CAGRs for the ILF ratios suggest that the growth rates for higher-limit policies are 2 to 4 percent higher—or 7 to 9 percent. Such growth rates are consistent with the 8.5-percent CAGR found for commercial trucking trial awards between 2010 and 2019 (see Table 5.2 in Chapter 5).

ILF ratios also grew little between 2012 and 2015 for CGL claims (see Figure 6.10). BI claims account for approximately 70 percent of CGL, premises and operations claims: The CAGR between 2015 and 2019 for these claims was not much different than those for the types of policyholders that tend to have low-severity claims (low-severity classes). The ILF ratio growth rates for mid-severity classes between 2015 and 2019 were again in the 2-to-3-percent range and were in the 1-to-2-percent range for high-severity classes.[6]

For CGL, products and completed operations claims, there was little growth in ILF ratios between 2012 and 2015 and limited or even negative growth between 2015 and 2019 (see Figure 6.11). BI claims account for only 40 percent of CGL, products and completed operations claims. These lower growth rates parallel the low growth rates in inflation-adjusted severity between 2010 and 2019 for $1 million/$2 million limit policies for both BI and PD claims in the CGL, products and completed operations market segment.

Discussion

Table 6.7 collects the findings from the analysis in this chapter, and the first row shows that after adjusting for inflation, the claim severity of BI claims across four market segments grew at a 2.7 percent CAGR between 2010 and 2019. These results apply to commercial BI policies and personal auto policies that typically have baseline policy limits (i.e., $1 million/$2 million and $100,000/$3000,000, respectively). The pattern of growth for BI claim severity lines up with that for inflation-adjusted trial awards in PI/WD cases. In both situations, there was little growth between 2010 and 2013, then faster growth from 2014 through 2019.

The 2.7-percent CAGR for BI inflation-adjusted claim severity is less than one-half of the 7.6-percent CAGR for PI/WD trial awards (see Table 5.1 in Chapter 5). The procedures that Verisk uses to calculate claim severity may, in part, account for this difference: Data from the previous five to seven years are used to develop reported losses, which means that if social inflation is accelerating, it may only gradually be reflected in the calculated claim severities.

---

[5] This can be expressed as $pc(AB) = pc(A) + pc(B) + (pc(A) \times pc(B))/100$, where *pc* stands for percentage change. If the product of $pc(A)$ and $pc(B)$ is less than 50, then the error induced by ignoring the last term is less than 0.5 of a percentage point.

[6] *Low-severity* business classes are those in roughly the bottom quartile in terms of severity, *mid-severity* classes are in the middle 50 percent, and *high-severity* classes are in the top quartile.

Figure 6.10
CAGRs for ILF Ratios for CGL, Premises and Operations Claims, by Policyholder Class

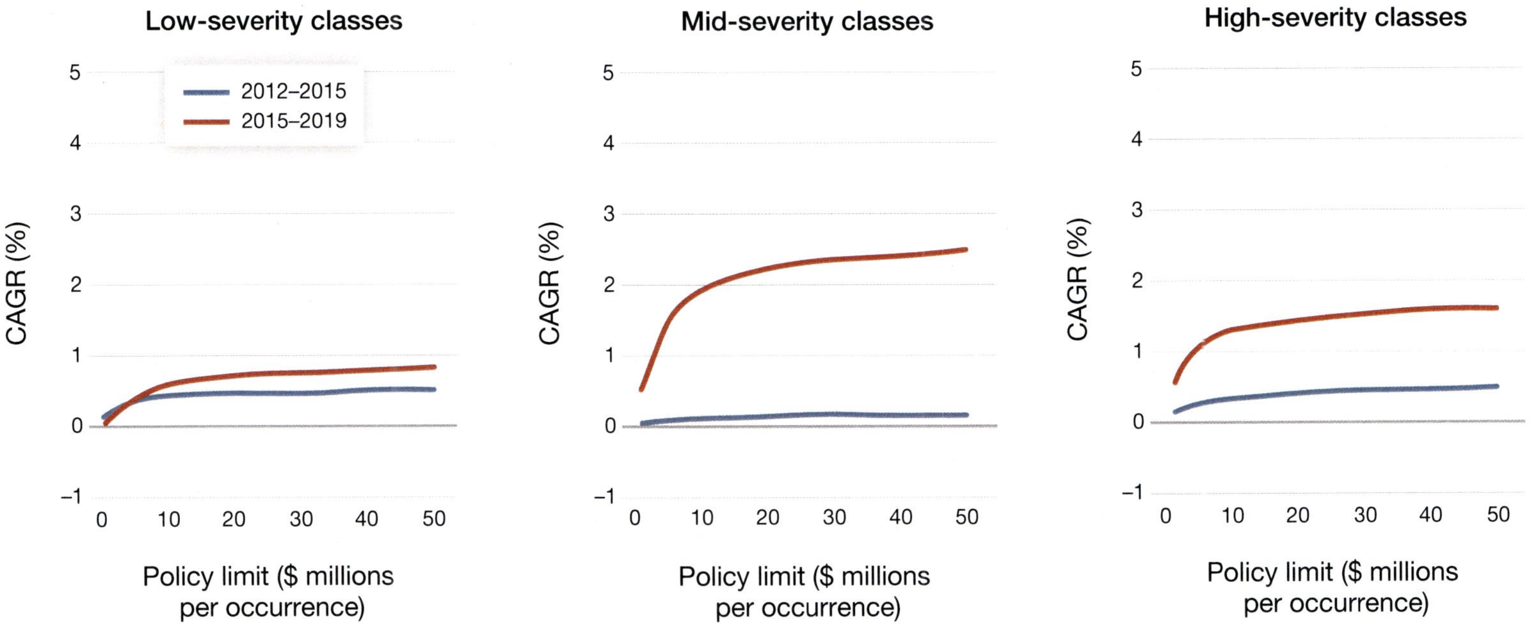

SOURCE: Authors' analysis of Verisk data.

FIGURE 6.11

CAGRs for ILF Ratios for CGL, Products and Completed Operations Claims, by Policyholder Class

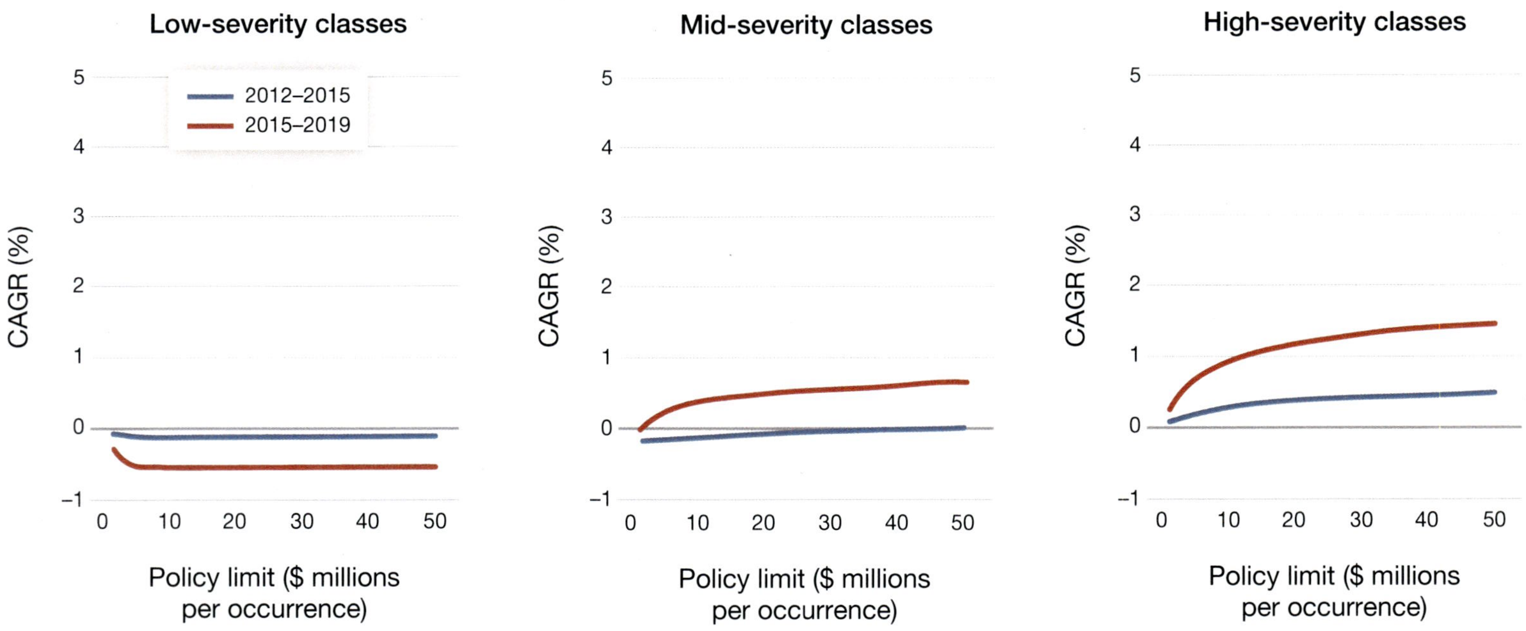

SOURCE: Authors' analysis of Verisk data.

TABLE 6.7

Summary of Findings on CAGRs for the Inflation-Adjusted Severity of Commercial Liability and Personal Auto Claims for Baseline Policy Limits

	Insurance Claims		
Market Segment	CAGR 2001–2010 (%)	CAGR 2010–2019 (%)	CAGR for Most Comparable Trial Award Subset, 2010–2019 (%)
BI claims	2.0[a]	2.7	7.4
CGL, premises and operations	0.9	4.3	8.6
CGL, products and completed operations	4.7	1.7	8.6
Third-party personal auto	—	2.0	8.3
Third-party commercial auto	0.5	3.0	5.8
Commercial auto—trucks, tractors, and trailers[b]	1.1	4.5	8.3
Commercial auto—private passenger vehicle types[b]	0.2	5.4	5.0
PD claims			
Including personal auto	—	3.5	—
Excluding personal auto	0.9	3.8	—

SOURCE: Authors' analysis of Verisk data.
NOTE: This table shows rates for claims brought under commercial liability policies with limits that are typically $1 million/$2 million and claims brought under personal auto policies with limits that usually do not exceed $100,000/$300,000.

[a] Excludes personal auto claims.

[b] Includes some PD claims.

In addition, small- and medium-sized businesses hold the policies on which the claim severities are typically based. We found that severity was increasing more rapidly for higher-limit policies and that, in some market segments, these growth rates were similar to those for trial awards. This result can be interpreted in various ways. On the one hand, it could indicate that social inflation affects higher-limit policies (and the large firms that typically hold them) to a greater degree than lower-limit policies. On the other hand, it could signal that social inflation affects all firms equally, no matter their policies' limits, but that increasingly binding policy limits reduce the growth rate that is observed for lower-limit policies. In this case, it could be that small- and medium-sized businesses with lower-limit policies experience the same effects of social inflation as large businesses with higher-limit policies do, while seeing constrained growth in insured losses that is offset by higher growth in uninsured losses.

These findings provide some initial evidence that the increase in claim severity might be driven, at least in part, by social inflation. As in the case of trial awards, however, these results are not conclusive. The annual growth in claim severity is volatile, and estimates of CAGRs are subject to considerable uncertainty. Changes in the medical treatment and health care practices that affect the quantity of medical care provided can increase claim costs absent social inflation, although initial sensitivity analysis suggests that such an effect does not have a major impact on our estimates. Finally, as we discuss in the next chapter, claim frequency decreased during the study period, potentially changing the mix of claims and increasing the severity of claims that remain.

Contrary to expectations, we found only limited evidence that the growth rates for PD claims were lower than those for BI claims. The growth rates were similar for the baseline policy limits; however, it could be that increasing binding limits for both types of claims limited the difference in growth rates. There are two pieces of information that provide some support for the notion that PD claims were not affected by social inflation to the same extent that BI claims were. First, we observed no upswing in severity growth rates for PD claims that corresponds to the increase in PI/WD trial awards beginning in 2014. Second, in contrast to the other market segments considered, ILF ratios show little uptick in growth between 2016 and 2019 for CGL, products and completed operations claims. Losses in this market segment were more heavily weighted toward property damage than in the other lines used for ILF analysis (60 percent versus 30 percent), suggesting that PD claims were less affected by social inflation. Further work on the factors driving the growth in PD claims is warranted. In particular, more detailed analysis on whether the price indices used for motor vehicle claims adequately control for changes in repair costs would be worthwhile.

CHAPTER 7

Trends in Insurance Claim Frequency and Loss Ratio

Analyses of social inflation seldom focus on changes in the frequency of insurance claims, but changes in frequency are relevant to better understanding the impacts of social inflation. Changes in frequency can either compound or offset the increase in inflation-adjusted claim severity (documented in Chapter 6) of the loss ratio for the underlying insurance policy. An increase in the loss ratio puts upward pressure on insurance premiums; thus, trends in claim frequency are critical to understanding whether social inflation might be expected to result in observed increases in premiums.

In this chapter, we first examine changes in on-level claim frequency over the study period. Recall from Chapter 3 that Verisk measures frequency in terms of the number of claims per million dollars of premium earned. On-level frequency corrects for changes in exposure and rates over time. We then examine changes in the real, on-level loss ratio. The real, on-level loss ratio is the product of the on-level frequency and inflation-adjusted severity.

Trends in Claim Frequency

On-level claim frequency decreased over the study period for all market segments examined. The CAGRs for the on-level frequency of commercial policies predominantly with $1 million/$2 million limits and personal auto policies with limits that typically do not exceed $100,000/$300,000 are shown in Table 7.1. As Table 7.1 shows,

- growth rates are negative between 2001 and 2010 for all those market segments with data available from 2001
- between 2010 and 2019, only the on-level frequency for third-party commercial auto BI claims increased—the on-level frequency for the other market segments all trended downward
- growth rates between 2001 and 2019 are all negative for those market segments with data available from 2001.

These negative growth rates resulted in considerable declines in claim frequency. Figure 7.1 shows the decline in on-level frequency for the BI market segments. The on-level frequency

TABLE 7.1
CAGRs for the On-Level Claim Frequency for Baseline Policy Limits

Market Segment	CAGR 2001–2010 (%)	CAGR 2010–2019 (%)	CAGR 2001–2019 (%)
BI claims			
CGL, premises and operations	−2.2***	−2.1***	−1.8***
CGL, products and completed operations	−7.1***	−5.2***	−4.9***
Third-party commercial auto	−4.7***	1.7***	−1.7***
Third-party personal auto	—	−1.2	—
PD claims			
CGL, premises and operations	−4.3***	−2.4***	−3.1***
CGL, products and completed operations	−1.8**	−1.2	−1.7***
Third-party commercial auto	−4.6***	−0.6**	−2.8***
Third-party personal auto	—	−1.7*	—
First-party commercial auto	−5.3***	−1.0***	−2.4***
First-party personal auto	—	−1.8*	—
Commercial property	−7.8***	−4.3***	−5.0***

SOURCE: Authors' analysis of Verisk data.
NOTE: This table shows rates for claims brought under commercial liability policies with limits that are typically $1 million/$2 million and claims brought under personal auto policies with limits that usually do not exceed $100,000/$300,000. * = statistically different from 0 with 90-percent probability; ** = statistically different from 0 with 95-percent probability; *** = statistically different from 0 with 99-percent probability.

for CGL, premises and operations BI claims dropped by nearly 40 percent between 2001 and 2019, and the on-level frequency for CGL, products and completed operations BI claims dropped by approximately 65 percent. Even though the frequency of third-party commercial auto BI claims remained fairly steady in the 2010s, the frequency of such claims in 2019 was still about 30 percent lower than it was in 2001.

Trends in Loss Ratio

Trends in the inflation-adjusted, on-level loss ratio for the examined market segments are presented in Table 7.2. Like in our other analyses using claims data, we calculated the loss ratios by accident year. The loss ratios all fell between 2001 and 2010. With the exception of CGL, products and completed operations, the loss ratios for all other market segments increased between 2010 and 2019, with the largest growth rate (4.7 percent) in third-party commercial auto BI claims. These increases presumably put some upward pressure on pre-

FIGURE 7.1

Trends in On-Level Frequency for BI Claims, by Market Segment

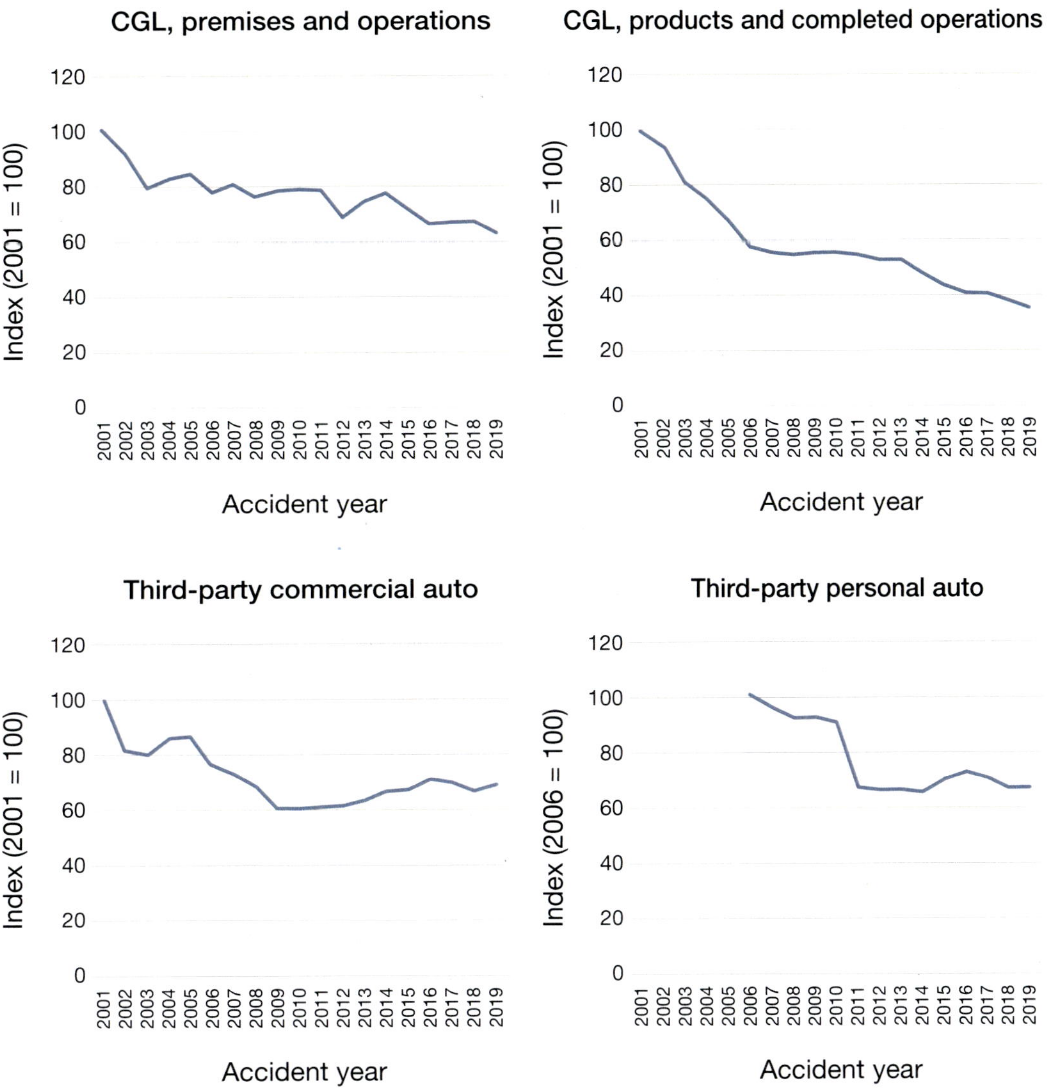

SOURCE: Authors' analysis of Verisk data.

TABLE 7.2
CAGRs for the Inflation-Adjusted, On-Level Loss Ratios for Baseline Policy Limits

Market Segment	CAGR 2001–2010 (%)	CAGR 2010–2019 (%)	CAGR 2001–2019 (%)
BI claims			
CGL, premises and operations	−1.3**	2.1***	0.3
CGL, products and completed operations	−2.7	−3.6***	−2.8***
Third-party commercial auto	−4.2***	4.7***	0.03
Third-party personal auto	—	0.8	—
PD claims			
CGL, premises and operations	−3.5***	1.3**	−1.5***
CGL, products and completed operations	−2.3**	0.6	−1.9***
Third-party commercial auto	−5.6***	2.7***	−1.7***
Third-party personal auto	—	1.4	—
First-party commercial auto	−3.5***	1.6***	−0.6*
First-party personal auto	—	0.8	—
Commercial property	−4.7	2.9**	−1.1

SOURCE: Authors' analysis of Verisk data.
NOTE: This table shows rates for claims brought under commercial liability policies with limits that are typically $1 million/$2 million and claims brought under personal auto policies with limits that usually do not exceed $100,000/$300,000. * = statistically different from 0 with 90-percent probability; ** = statistically different from 0 with 95-percent probability; *** = statistically different from 0 with 99-percent probability.

miums between 2010 and 2019. However, the inflation-adjusted, on-level ratio declined or increased at very moderate rates between 2001 and 2019 for all the market segments for which calculations could be made (see last column of Table 7.2).

Discussion

The declines in on-level frequency between 2001 and 2019 were large enough to nearly or fully offset the increase in severity for all the market segments considered. Between 2010 and 2019, declines in frequency partially offset the increase in severity, with the exception of third-party commercial auto BI claims. In this case, an increase in frequency compounded the increase in severity.

As discussed in Chapter 2, social inflation could lead individuals to seek compensation for injuries more frequently, thus increasing the frequency of insurance claims. However, increased safety regulation can reduce the underlying injury rate. By increasing liability costs, social inflation itself can also induce potentially responsible parties to improve safety practices and reduce the underlying injury rate.[1] Consequently, a decline in insurance claim frequency does not mean that social inflation is not occurring. Such a decline only means that social inflation will not necessarily manifest as an increase in observed loss ratios or insurance premiums. It could be the case, however, that loss ratios and premiums would have declined more rapidly absent social inflation.

The declines in claim frequency reported in this chapter contrast with the increase in tort filings per capita found in Chapter 3. One potential explanation for the increase in filings per capita is that the underlying tortious incidents are increasing. The declines in claim frequency provide some support for the hypothesis that the increase in tort filing per capita is driven, at least in part, by social inflation and not primarily by an increase in underlying tortious incidents.

The substantial declines in claim frequency raise another issue that merits attention. It is possible that large declines could affect the mix of claims, potentially leading to an increase in severity even in the absence of social inflation. Further investigation of this possibility is warranted.

---

[1] Claim frequency could, in principle, decline if policy deductibles were rising. However, deductibles are uncommon in liability policies, and according to a Verisk representative, deductibles on PD policies have not changed a great deal over the period examined (Verisk representative, discussion with the authors, 2023).

CHAPTER 8

Implications

Our starting point for investigating the extent and impact of social inflation was to determine whether there is evidence of outcomes consistent with the expected effects of social inflation. To that end, we assembled and analyzed data on litigation trends, verdicts, and insurance claims.

We found evidence consistent with the expected effects of social inflation as follows:

- **Case filings per capita increased.** The annual number of new tort case filings per capita rose about 10 percent between 2012 and 2019 in 19 states for which data were available.
- **Plaintiff win rate rose.** The plaintiff win rate rose considerably over the study period and across all the case types examined.
- **Trial awards increased.** After adjusting for inflation, awards per plaintiff rose at an average 7.6-percent CAGR between 2010 and 2019. Trial awards began increasing in 2014, consistent with stakeholder experience and the increased use of the term "social inflation" online. These findings are sensitive to the indices used to control for medical care cost inflation, but growth rates remain considerable under plausible scenarios that consider changes in both the price and quantity of medical expenditures.
- **Insurance claim severity rose.** The inflation-adjusted severity of commercial insurance BI claims brought under policies that typically have $1 million/$2 million limits and personal auto policies with limits that do not exceed $100,000/$300,000 rose at a CAGR of approximately 3.5 percent between 2010 and 2019. Severity appears to have increased at faster rates for higher-limit policies in several market segments.
- **The pattern of growth in the severity of BI insurance claims mirrored that for trial awards.** In both cases, there was little growth between 2010 and 2013, followed by moderate growth from 2014 through 2019.

The findings, however, do not always line up with the expected impacts of social inflation. First, we did not find evidence that organizational entities were more heavily affected than non-organizational entities. However, our analyses did not consider the size of organizational defendants. One possible interpretation of the faster growth in severity for higher-limit policies is that social inflation has a greater impact on the large firms that typically hold them. Second, the relatively steady increase in the plaintiff win rate over the study period does not align with the jump in trial awards in the second half of the 2010s. Finally, we found only limited evidence that insurance severity for lower-limit policies grew more slowly for PD claims than for BI claims. Further work on the factors driving the growth in PD claims is warranted. In particular, more detailed analysis of whether the price indices used for motor vehicle claims adequately control for changes in repair cost would be worthwhile.

We also found that frequency of insurance claims decreased considerably over the study period. A decline in claim frequency does not necessarily imply that social inflation is not occurring, but such a decline indicates that social inflation will not necessarily manifest as an observed increase in loss ratios or insurance premiums. It could be the case, however, that loss ratios and premiums would have declined more rapidly absent social inflation.

We did not attempt to formally isolate social inflation from other factors that could be causing inflation-adjusted trial awards and insurance claim severity to increase. As discussed in the preceding chapters, there are many plausible and competing explanations for each of the trends observed. However, the findings in this report provide initial information consistent with the potential surge of social inflation during the 2010s.

Further work in the following areas would help to develop a better understanding of whether social inflation exists and its magnitude:

- The statistical power of our insurance claim analysis is limited by having access to only average claim severity across all claims in a given year by market segment. Additional insights and precision in the estimate of the consequences of social inflation would likely be gained by using claim-level data.
- An understanding of the trends in claim frequency and severity for higher-limit policies, including those in the excess and surplus lines markets, would improve insight into whether social inflation is affecting larger firms more than smaller firms.
- An examination of the relationship between changes in claim severity and the tort regime or tactics of the plaintiffs' attorneys in each state could also prove a fruitful area for analysis. Variation in tort standards, damage caps, and litigation practices by the plaintiffs' bars across states and their changes over time could help better isolate and quantify the effects of social inflation.
- Further investigation of how best to control for changes in medical practice patterns and the price and quality of vehicle replacement parts would provide more confidence on the extent to which increases in trial awards and claim severity are caused by social inflation or to factors external to the tort system.

The findings in this report contribute to evidence that social inflation has occurred in some insurance lines. Concluding that social inflation exists is not an assessment about whether it is good or bad—that will depend on the factors driving it. For example, one could argue that an increase of trial awards because jurors are ignoring the law or insurance contract language is a negative driver of social inflation. Conversely, elimination of a cap on noneconomic damages by legislative action could be viewed as a positive driver consistent with broader public will. A next step in the assessment of social inflation is to gain a better understanding of the factors that are driving it and whether these factors serve broader social goals.

Statistical Methods and Sensitivity Analysis

In this appendix, we describe the statistical methods used to estimate the outcomes of interest in our analysis: plaintiff win rate, trial awards, insurance claim severity, and claim frequency and loss ratio. We also report the sensitivity of the results to trimming the largest and smallest trial awards, as well as to the price indices used to adjust for inflation.

Changes in Plaintiff Win Rate

The change in the plaintiff win rate over the study period, controlling for case characteristics, was estimated using the following equation:

$$Prob(pwin_i) = f(casetype_i; wrongfuldeath_i; state_i; year_i) \quad \text{(A.1)}$$

where

- i = verdict
- $pwin_i$ = indicator of whether the plaintiff received a monetary award in verdict i
- $casetype_i$ = categorical variable for the case type of verdict i
- $wrongfuldeath_i$ = categorical variable indicating whether the case involved a WD claim
- $state_i$ = categorical variable for the state in which verdict i was reached
- $year_i$ = categorical or continuous variable for the year in which verdict i was reached (2010 to 2019).

Equation A.1 is estimated using Stata's logit command, with plaintiff win being the positive outcome. The extent of brain injury is excluded from the logit because social inflation may influence the tendency of plaintiffs to seek recovery for alleged brain injuries. The coefficients on the year variable when expressed in categorical form measure the change in the plaintiff win rate (in percentage points) in the indicated year relative to the reference year (2010). Stata's margins command is used to calculate the estimated change in the plaintiff win rate relative to 2010 for each year.[1] To estimate the growth rate over the study period in

[1] The Stata commands are (1) *logit* pwin i.casetype i.wrongfuldeath, i.state i.year and (2) margins <year variable in categorical form>.

percentage points per year, the year variable is specified as a continuous variable with values from 2010 through 2019. The Stata margins command is used to calculate the annual percentage point change and standard error from this second version of the estimated logit.[2]

Growth in Trial Awards

The change in trial awards over the study period conditional on a positive award is estimated using the following equation:

$$ln(award_i) = f(casetype_i;\ wrongfuldeath_i;\ state_i;\ year_i) \qquad (A.2)$$

where *ln* is the natural logarithm and *i* indexes trial awards. Stata's regress command is used to estimate the model, using year expressed as a categorical variable to indicate how award level in year *t* compares with 2010 and year expressed as a continuous variable to estimate the CAGR. A nonlinear transformation is used to convert the coefficient on year into percentage point changes.[3]

We examined the coefficients on year when it is expressed as a categorical variable to determine if and when there appears to be a marked increase in award amounts. The size and statistical significance of the estimated coefficient were considered in making this determination. To estimate the growth rate prior to the year in which there was a marked increase, we reran regression (2), restricting observations to plaintiff wins reached between 2010 and the year preceding the increase. We needed a baseline period on which to calculate estimates of the growth rate after the increase. We used all awards prior to the increase for the baseline period and reset the continuous year variable to the midpoint of this period. For example, if the increase occurred in 2014, the baseline period includes awards between 2010 and 2013. The year variable is reset to 2011.5 for the verdicts in this subperiod, and the regression is rerun using the whole sample.

Table A.1 shows the coefficients for the regression used to estimate the CAGR for all trial awards from 2010 through 2019. We exclude the extent of brain damage from Specification 1 (which is the specification used to estimate the growth rates reported in Chapter 5) because social inflation may affect the frequency with which brain injuries are alleged. In Table A.1, we also report the results when brain damage is included in the regression.

---

2 The Stata commands are (1) *logit* pwin i.casetype i.wrongfuldeath, i.state year and (2) margins, dydx(<year variable in continuous form>).

3 The Stata commands are (1) *regress* ln(award) i.casetype i.wrongfuldeath, i.state i.year when year is in a categorical variable form and (2) *regress* ln(award) i.casetype i.wrongfuldeath, i.state year when year is in a continuous variable form. The estimates are converted to CAGRs using *nlcom* (exp(_b[year]) – 1) × 100, where _b[year] references the regression coefficient on year, and year is a continuous variable. The growth between year *t* and year (*t*–1) is calculated using *nlcom* (exp(_b[year(*t*)] – _b[year(*t*–1)]) – 1) × 100, where _b[year] references the regression coefficient on year, and year is a categorical variable.

TABLE A.1

Linear Regression Results for Natural Logarithm of Inflation-Adjusted Trial Awards per Plaintiff

	Specification 1		Specification 2	
Case Characteristic	**Coefficient**	**Standard Error**	**Coefficient**	**Standard Error**
Case type				
Commercial trucking	Reference	—	Reference	—
Other commercial auto	−0.914***	0.083	−0.834***	0.082
Personal auto	−2.197***	0.076	−2.055***	0.075
Medical malpractice	0.975***	0.097	0.950***	0.095
Other cases against organizational defendants	0.206***	0.079	0.293***	0.078
Other cases against non-organizational defendants	−1.111***	0.104	−0.993***	0.102
State fixed effects	Omitted		Omitted	
Claimed harm				
Personal injury	Reference	—	Reference	—
Wrongful death	1.316***	0.061	1.264***	0.060
Extent of brain injury				
None	Reference	—	Reference	—
Other	—	—	0.169***	0.056
Serious	—	—	1.309***	0.056
Year	0.073***	0.006	0.064***	0.006
Constant	−134.362***	11.733	−115.983***	11.607
N	15,017		15,017	
Adjusted R^2	0.437		0.457	

NOTE: * = statistically different from 0 with 90-percent probability; ** = statistically different from 0 with 95-percent probability; *** = statistically different from 0 with 99-percent probability.

This regression can be interpreted as an estimate for CAGR while holding the extent of brain injury constant. When the extent of brain injury is excluded, the CAGR is 7.6 percent (exp(0.072837) − 1) × 100). When it is included, the CAGR is 6.6 percent, indicating that the increasing prevalence of brain injuries does not account for a substantial share of the CAGRs between 2010 and 2019.

Growth in Insurance Claim Severity

We used a similar approach to estimate the CAGRs for insurance claim severity. In this case, severities of each of the market segments considered were stacked and the growth rate calculated using the following relationship:

$$ln(severity_{mt}) = f(market\_segment_m; year_t) \tag{A.3}$$

where m indexes the market segment and t indexes the accident year; $severity_{mt}$ is the average severity of claims in market segment m and accident year t.

Trends in Insurance Claim Frequency and Loss Ratio

We separately calculated the CAGRs for on-level frequency for each market segment by regressing the natural logarithm of the on-level frequency on a constant and year expressed as a continuous variable. The resulting estimates were transformed using the Stata *nlcom* command. We used the same approach to calculate the CAGRs for the inflation-adjusted on-level loss ratio.

Sensitivity of Estimated Trial Award Growth Rates to Outliers

Analysis of regression residuals for Equation A.2 indicates that the tails of the error distribution are heavy compared with a normal distribution.[4] A relatively small number of very large awards cause the right tail to be fatter than the normal, and we used the Winsorization approach to examine the sensitivity of the results to outliers.[5] Figure A.1 compares the mean of the full sample of trial awards before and after Winsorization.

Once the data are Winsorized, the regression residuals for Equation A.2 no longer appear to have heavier tails than the normal distribution. As shown in Table A.2, estimates of the annual growth rate in trial awards are not overly sensitive to a 5-percent Winsorization. The annual growth rate for all awards declines from 7.6 to 7.0 percent. The annual growth rates

---

[4] This analysis is done using Stata's *qnorm* and *pnorm* commands.

[5] *Winsorization* is a statistical technique that limits extreme values in order to reduce, but not eliminate, the effect of outliers. In a Winsorized dataset, values outside a particular percentile are set equal to that percentile. For example, a 5-percent Winsorization would involve setting any value below the 2.5th percentile to the 2.5th percentile and any value above the 97.5th percentile to the 97.5th percentile. The 5-percent Winsorized data are generated using the following Stata command: *winsor* <varname>, gen(<new_varname>) p(0.025). A 5-percent Winsorization has the most effect on the roughly 2 percent of awards that are greater than or equal to $50 million in our dataset.

FIGURE A.1

Trial Award per Plaintiff for Plaintiff Wins in PI/WD Tort Cases

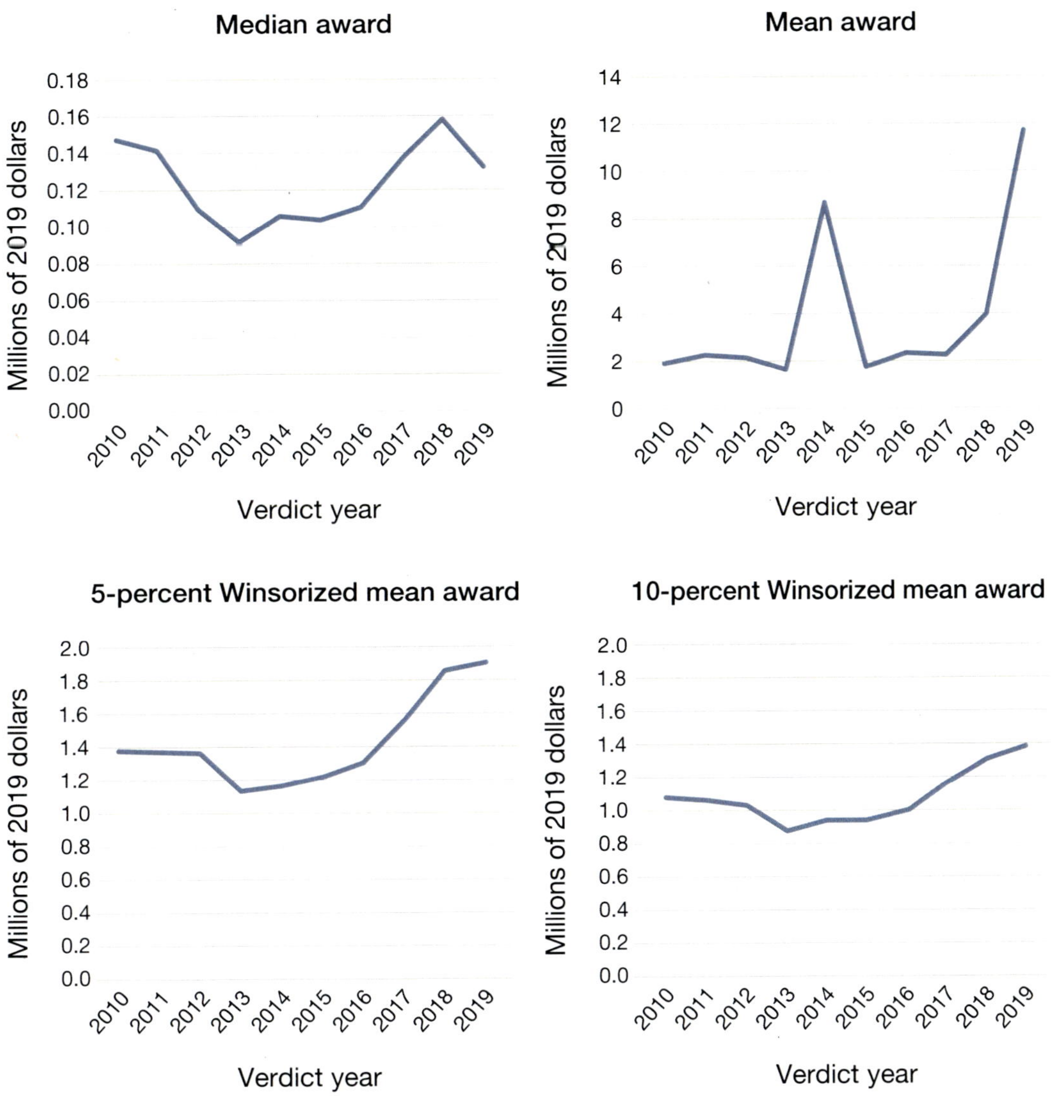

SOURCE: Authors' analysis of 2010–2019 VerdictSearch data.
NOTE: *N* = 15,017 trial awards.

for each case type also do not show particularly large declines.[6] The largest decline is for other cases against organizational defendants, which drops from 8.8 percent to 7.5 percent.

[6] Winsorization is done separately for each case type. For example, when the 683 commercial trucking awards were analyzed, Winsorization used each of these 683 observations and not the entire sample of 15,017 awards.

TABLE A.2

Sensitivity of CAGR Estimates for Inflation-Adjusted Trial Awards per Plaintiff to a 5-Percent Winsorization

	Reported Trial Awards		5-Percent Winsorized Awards	
Award Subset	CAGR 2010–2019 (%)	Year Growth Rate Accelerated	CAGR 2010–2019 (%)	Year Growth Rate Accelerated
All awards	7.6***	2014	7.0***	2014
Organizational defendants				
Commercial trucking	8.5***	2018	8.4***	2018
Other commercial vehicles	5.1***	2017	4.7***	2017
Medical malpractice	5.7**	2018	5.3**	2018
Other cases against organizational defendants	8.8***	2014	7.5***	2014
Non-organizational defendants				
Private auto	8.3***	2014	8.1***	2014
Other cases against non-organizational defendants	8.1**	2016	7.2**	2016

SOURCE: Authors' analysis of 2010–2019 VerdictSearch data.
NOTE: * = statistically different from 0 with 90-percent probability; ** = statistically different from 0 with 95-percent probability; *** = statistically different from 0 with 99-percent probability.

Sensitivity of Estimates to Price Indices

We used the PCEPI to adjust trial awards for economic inflation. Although the PCEPI has a medical care component, as a price index, the PCEPI does not consider changes in the quantity of medical care consumed. Increases in the quantity of health care consumed because of factors outside the tort system would reduce the portion of the overall increase in trial awards that could be attributed to social inflation. To understand how changes in medical practice patterns might affect the results, we used data on annual U.S. health expenditures per capita.[7] As Figure A.2 shows, the annual percentage change in per capita health expenditures is considerably higher than that for the medical care component of the PCEPI.

We used a weighted average of the PCEPI and an index for annual U.S. health expenditures per capita to adjust trial awards for economic inflation and changes in medical practice patterns. The CAGRs for trial awards using various weights are shown in Table A.3. The first row replicates the results from the baseline case presented in Chapter 5. In this baseline case, only the PCEPI was used to adjust trial awards.

[7] See Centers for Medicare and Medicaid Services, "National Health Expenditure Data: Historical," webpage, December 13, 2023.

FIGURE A.2

Comparison of Year-Over-Year Percentage Change in the PCEPI Medical Care Component and U.S. Health Expenditures per Capita

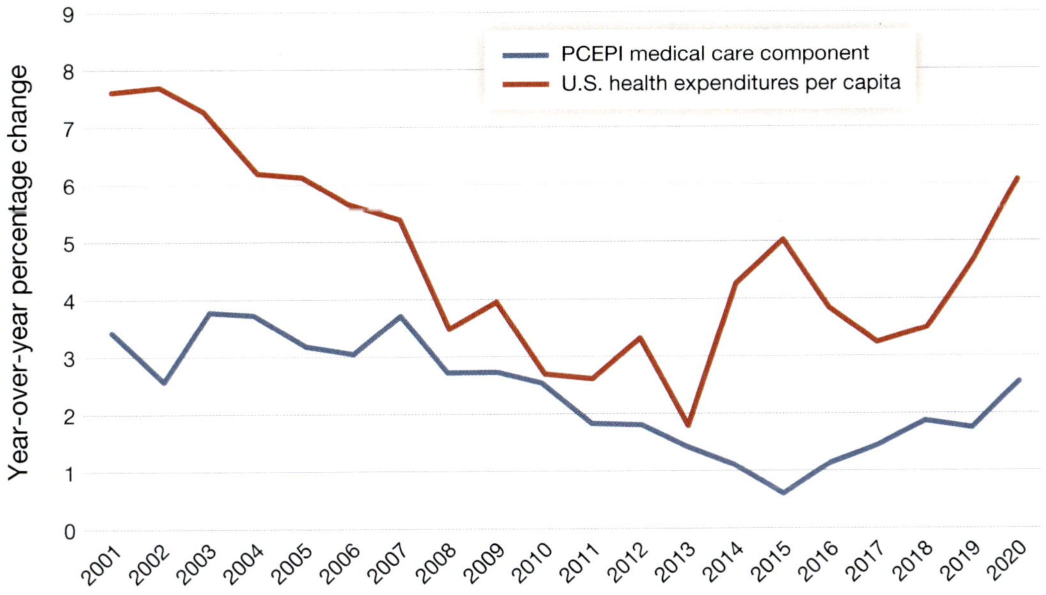

SOURCE: Authors' analysis using data from St. Louis Federal Reserve Bank, undated, and Centers for Medicare and Medicaid Services, 2023.

TABLE A.3

Sensitivity of the CAGRs for PI/WD Trial Awards per Plaintiff to Weighted Indices Used to Adjust for Inflation and Changes in Medical Practice Patterns

	Index Weights				CAGR (%)	
Scenario	PCEPI	U.S. Health Expenditures Index	CAGR 2010–2019 (%)	Year Growth Rate Increased	Pre-Dividing Point	Post-Dividing Point
Baseline case	1.00	0.00	7.6***	2014	−3.8*	8.0***
Version 2	0.75	0.25	7.0***	2014	−3.9*	7.5***
Version 3	0.50	0.50	6.4***	2014	−4.1*	6.9***
Version 4	0.25	0.75	5.9***	2014	−4.3**	6.3***
Version 5	0.00	1.00	5.2***	2014	−4.5**	5.6***

SOURCE: Authors' analysis of 2010–2019 VerdictSearch data.
NOTE: *N* = 15,017; * = statistically different from 0 with 90-percent probability; ** = statistically different from 0 with 95-percent probability; *** = statistically different from 0 with 99-percent probability.

To test the sensitivity of the estimated CAGRs for the severity of BI insurance claims, we replaced the PCEPI medical care component with the index for annual U.S. health expenditures per capita. Recall from Chapter 3 that the index used to adjust the severity of BI claims is the average of the PCEPI and the PCEPI medical care component. The second and fourth columns of Table A.4 repeat the results from Table 6.2 in Chapter 6. The third and fifth columns report the results of using the index of U.S. health expenditures per capita instead of the PCEPI medical care component.

TABLE A.4

Sensitivity of the CAGRs for Inflation-Adjusted Severity of BI Claims to the Index Used to Adjust for Inflation and Changes in Medical Practice Patterns

	Includes Personal Auto[a]		Excludes Personal Auto[b]	
Period	Baseline Case	Using U.S. Health Expenditures Index	Baseline Case	Using U.S. Health Expenditures Index
2010–2013	−0.4	−0.8	−0.8	−1.2
2014–2019	3.5***	2.3***	3.8***	2.5***

SOURCE: Authors' analysis of 2010–2019 VerdictSearch data.

NOTE: * = statistically different from 0 with 90-percent probability; ** = statistically different from 0 with 95-percent probability; *** = statistically different from 0 with 99-percent probability.

[a] Based on annual observations of severity between 2010 and 2019 for the following four market segments: CGL, premises and operations; CGL, products and completed operations; third-party commercial auto; and third-party personal auto.

[b] Based on annual observations of severity between 2010 and 2019 for the following three market segments: CGL, premises and operations; CGL, products and completed operations; and third-party commercial auto.

Additional Statistics on Verdicts and Trial Awards

As shown in Figure B.1, the breakdown of trial verdicts by case type varied somewhat between 2010 and 2019 but was fairly stable. The percentages of commercial trucking,

FIGURE B.1
Distribution of Verdicts, by Case Type, 2010–2019

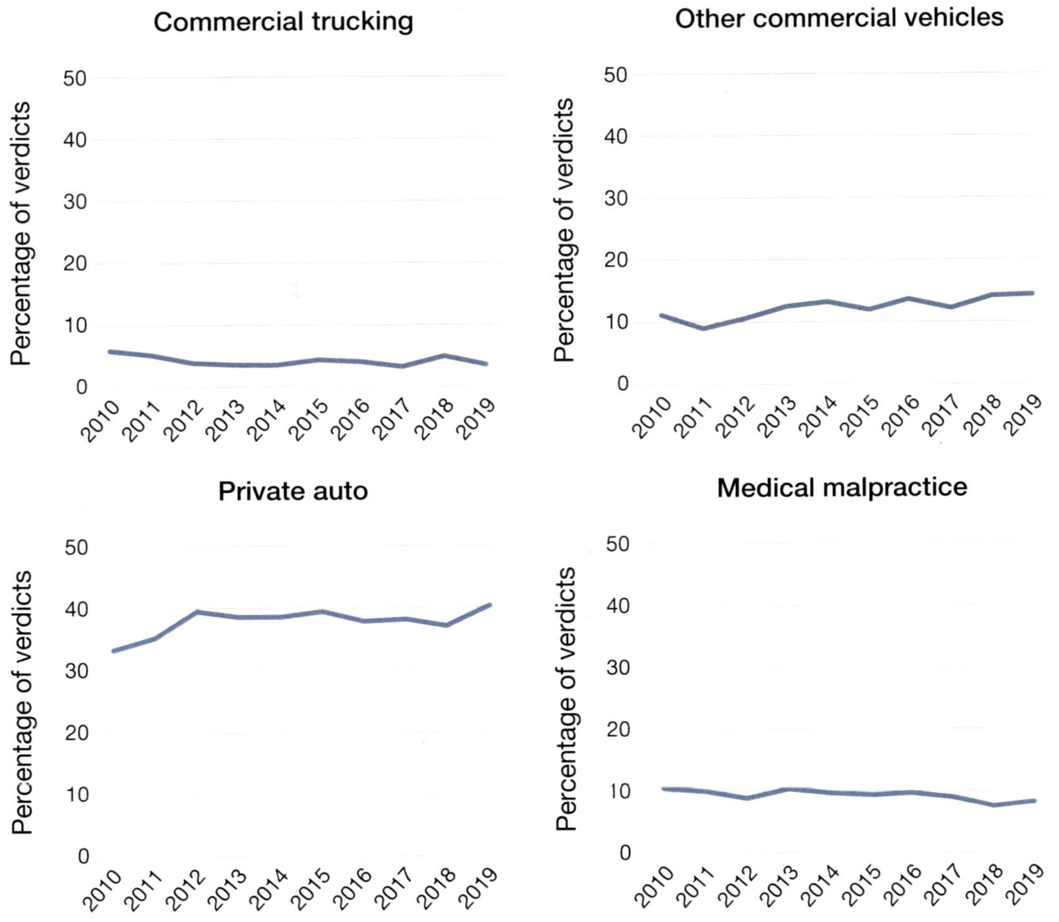

Figure B.1—Continued

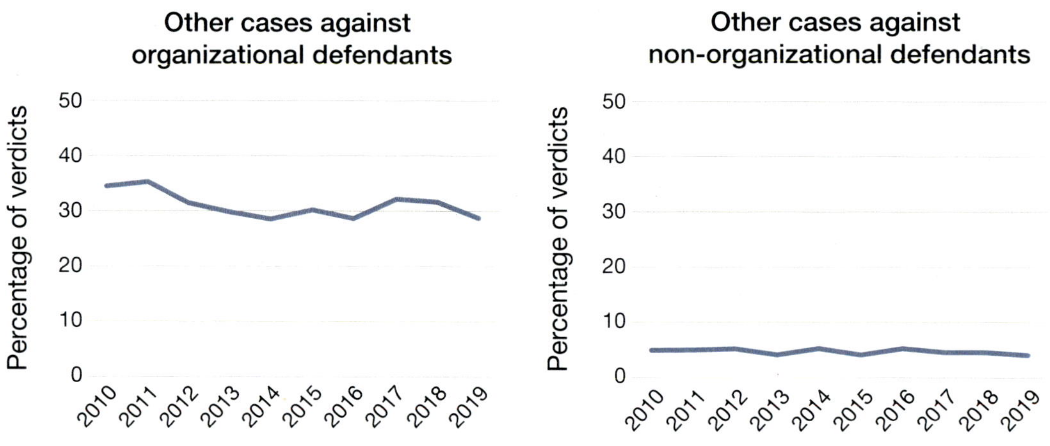

SOURCE: Authors' analysis of 2010–2019 VerdictSearch data.
NOTE: *N* = 26,114 trial awards.

medical malpractice, and other cases against organizational defendants tended to decline, while the percentages of other commercial auto and personal auto cases tended to increase.

The mean and median awards per plaintiff for the 15,017 verdicts with positive awards varied considerably by case characteristic (Table B.1). The median award across all trial awards was $140,000 in inflation-adjusted dollars. A relatively small number of larger awards brought the mean up to $7.38 million. The mean and median awards were highest for medical malpractice cases and lowest for private auto cases.

TABLE B.1

Mean and Median Trial Awards per Plaintiff in PI/WD Tort Cases

Case Characteristic	Number of Trial Awards	Trial Award per Plaintiff (millions of 2019 dollars)	
		Median	Mean
All trial awards	15,017	0.14	7.38
Case type			
Medical malpractice	888	1.79	8.67
Commercial trucking	683	0.48	3.88
Other commercial vehicles	2,235	0.15	2.24
Private auto	6,405	0.03	0.57
Other cases against organizational defendants	4,165	1.03	21.30
Other cases against non-organizational defendants	641	0.13	4.66
Claimed harm			
Bodily injury	13,808	0.11	4.15
Wrongful death	1,209	4.21	44.30
Brain injury indication			
Serious brain injury	1,288	2.06	13.00
Other brain injury	3,637	0.10	2.74
No brain injury	10,092	0.12	8.33
State			
California	2,013	0.37	4.93
Florida	1,465	0.53	25.20
Illinois	859	0.08	3.08
New Jersey	902	0.24	1.61
New York	2,451	0.33	2.94
Pennsylvania	1,156	0.08	9.46
Texas	3,171	0.02	1.98
All other states	3,000	0.13	11.80

SOURCE: Authors' analysis of 2010–2019 VerdictSearch data.

Abbreviations

ALAE	allocated loss adjustment expenses
BI	bodily injury
CAGR	compound annual growth rate
CGL	commercial general liability
ILF	increased limit factor
IRC	Insurance Research Council
NAIC	National Association of Insurance Commissioners
NCSC	National Center for State Courts
PCEPI	personal consumption expenditures price index
PD	property damage
PI	personal injury
TDI	Texas Department of Insurance
WD	wrongful death

References

ALM, homepage, undated-a. As of May 6, 2024:
https://www.alm.com/

ALM, "Law.com VerdictSearch: Featured Verdicts," webpage, undated-b. As of May 10, 2024:
https://www.law.com/verdictsearch/featured-verdicts/

Beardsley, Craig, Erin Collins, Tim Fletcher, Glenn Frankel, Andrew Gifford, and Tom Karol, *Social Inflation Is Complicated and Costly: A Five-Part Series Examining Social Inflation and Its Impact on Insurers*, National Association of Mutual Insurance Companies, NAMIC Issue Analysis, September 2021.

Bruton, Michael, "Identify Factors Contributing to Social Inflation," *DocLens.ai Blogs*, October 18, 2022.

Buffett, Warren, "Chairman's Letter—1977," Berkshire Hathaway, March 14, 1978. As of June 12, 2022:
https://www.berkshirehathaway.com/letters/1977.html

California Highway Patrol, "SWITRS 2019 Report: 2019 Annual Report of Fatal and Injury Motor Vehicle Traffic Crashes," webpage, undated. As of May, 16 2024:
https://www.chp.ca.gov/programs-services/services-information/switrs-internet-statewide-integrated-traffic-records-system/switrs-2019-report

Centers for Medicare and Medicaid Services, "National Health Expenditure Data: Historical," webpage, December 13, 2023. As of March 19, 2024:
https://www.cms.gov/data-research/statistics-trends-and-reports/national-health-expenditure-data/historical

Daniels, Stephen, and Joanne Martin, *Civil Juries and the Politics of Reform*, Northwestern University Press, August 1995.

Dixon, Lloyd, and Jamie Morikawa, *Improving the Availability and Affordability of Pandemic Risk Insurance: Projected Performance of Proposed Programs*, RAND Corporation, RR-A1223-1, 2021. As of May 16, 2024:
https://www.rand.org/pubs/research_reports/RRA1223-1.html

Federal Reserve Bank of St. Louis, "Table 2.4.4. Price Indexes for Personal Consumption Expenditures by Type of Product: Annual," FRED release, undated. As of November 30, 2022:
https://fred.stlouisfed.org/release/tables?rid=53&eid=44068#snid=44069

Florida Office of the State Courts Administrator, "Circuit Civil Overview," in *FY 2018–19 Statistical Reference Guide*, March 2020.

Galanter, Marc, "The Regulatory Function of the Civil Jury," in Robert E. Litan, ed., *Verdict: Assessing the Civil Jury System*, Brookings Institution Press, 1993.

Gibson, S., B. Harris, N. Waters, K. Genthon, M. Hamilton, E. Bailey Stevens, M. Moffett, and D. Robinson, eds., "CSP STAT Civil," Court Statistics Project database, National Center for State Courts and Conference of State Court Administrators, October 9, 2023. As of May 17, 2024:
https://www.courtstatistics.org/court-statistics/interactive-caseload-data-displays/csp-stat-nav-cards-first-row/csp-stat-civil

Google Ngram Viewer Team, "About Ngram Viewer," webpage, undated. As of May 2, 2024:
https://books.google.com/ngrams/info

Hannaford-Agor, Paula, Scott Graves, and Shelley Spacek Miller, *The Landscape of Civil Litigation in State Courts*, National Center for State Courts, 2015.

Hannaford-Agor, Paula, Robert C. LaFountain, and Shauna Strickland, "Trial Trends and Implications for the Civil Justice System," *Caseload Highlights*, Vol. 11, No. 3, National Center for State Courts, June 2005.

"The Hartford Reports: More Than 40 Percent of Small Businesses Will Experience a Claim in the Next 10 Years," The Hartford, March 30, 2015.

Hunter, J. Robert, Joanne Doroshow, and Douglas Heller, *How the Cash-Rich Insurance Industry Fakes Crises and Invents Social Inflation*, Consumer Federation of America and the Center for Justice and Democracy at New York Law School, March 2020.

Insurance Research Council, *Social Inflation: Evidence and Impact on Property-Casualty Insurance*, June 2020.

IRC—*See* Insurance Research Council.

Janson, Wesley, Randal Verbrugge, and Carola Conces Binder, "The CPI-PCEPI Inflation Differential: Causes and Prospects," *Economic Commentary*, Federal Reserve Bank of Cleveland, Number 2020-06, March 2, 2020.

Judicial Council of California, *2021 Court Statistics Report: Statewide Caseload Trends 2010–11 Through 2019–20*, 2021.

Langton, Lynn, and Thomas H. Cohen, *Civil Bench and Jury Trials in State Courts, 2005*, Bureau of Justice Statistics Special Report, U.S. Department of Justice, October 2008, revised April 9, 2009.

Lynch, Jim, and Dave Moore, *Social Inflation and Loss Development*, Casualty Actuarial Society and Insurance Information Institute, 2022.

Oh, Sangmin, "Social Inflation," Social Science Research Network, October 5, 2021.

Pace, Nicholas M., Daniela Golinelli, and Laura Zakaras, *Capping Non-Economic Awards in Medical Malpractice Trials: California Jury Verdicts Under MICRA*, RAND Corporation, MG-234-ICJ, 2004. As of May 16, 2024:
https://www.rand.org/pubs/monographs/MG234.html

Pain, Darren, *Social Inflation: Navigating the Evolving Claims Environment*, Geneva Association, December 2020.

Rozanski, Keith M., "Keith Rozanski Moderating Panel Evaluating the Rise of Traumatic Brain Injury Allegations in Hospitality and Retail Personal Injury Claims," Haight, undated.

Sedgwick, "Liability, Litigation Trends, Drivers and Strategies," 2022.

Swiss Re Institute, "Social Inflation: A Building Pain Point in US Liability Insurance," *Economic Insights*, No. 21/2019, November 14, 2019.

Swiss Re Institute, *U.S. Litigation Funding and Social Inflation: The Rising Costs of Legal Liability*, December 2021.

TDI—*See* Texas Department of Insurance.

Texas Department of Insurance, *The 2012 Texas Liability Insurance Closed Claim Annual Report*, 2014.

U.S. Bureau of Economic Analysis, "Real Gross Domestic Product [GDPC1]," FRED database, Federal Reserve Bank of St. Louis, April 25, 2024. As of May 17, 2024:
https://fred.stlouisfed.org/series/GDPC1

U.S. Bureau of Labor Statistics, "Consumer Price Index: Quality Adjustment in the CPI," webpage, March 12, 2024. As of March 23, 2024:
https://www.bls.gov/cpi/quality-adjustment/home.htm

Verisk, "Information from the Verisk Database," webpage, undated. As of May 2, 2022:
https://www.verisk.com/insurance/capabilities/data-and-statistical-services/information-from-the-iso-database

"Walmart Settles Tracy Morgan Lawsuit After Deadly Crash with Company Truck," *The Guardian*, May 27, 2015.

Wilkinson, Claire, "Social Inflation Keeps Rising for Insurers: Panelists," *Business Insurance*, January 17, 2020.

World Bank, "Population, Total for United States [POPTOTUSA647NWDB]," FRED database, Federal Reserve Bank of St. Louis, July 4, 2023. As of May 17, 2024:
https://fred.stlouisfed.org/graph/?g=ji3R